The Getaway Guide
to the John Muir Trail

The Getaway Guide
to the John Muir Trail

Guy T. Saperstein

RDR Books
Berkeley, California

Getaway Guide to The John Muir Trail

RDR Books
2415 Woolsey
Berkeley, CA 94705
Phone: (510) 595-0595
Fax: (510) 228-0300
E-mail: read@rdrbooks.com
Website: www.rdrbooks.com

ISBN: 1-57143-098-9

Library of Congress Catalog Card Number 2005900471

Editor: Joanna Pearlman
Design, Production and Maps: Richard Harris
Photography: Guy T. Saperstein
Cover photo: *Fish Creek* by Guy T. Saperstein

Distributed in Canada by Jaguar Book Group c/o Fraser
Direct, 100 Armstrong Way, Georgetown, ON L7G 5S4

Distributed in the United Kingdom and Europe by
Roundhouse Publishing, Ltd., Millstone, Limers Lane,
Northam, North Deven EX39 2RG, United Kingdom

Printed in Canada by Transcontinental Printing

And after ten years spent in the heart of it, rejoicing and wondering, bathing in its glorious floods of light, seeing the sunbursts of morning among the icy peaks, the noon-day radiance on the trees and rocks and snow, the flush of the alpenglow, and a thousand dashing waterfalls with their marvelous abundance of irised spray, it still seems to me above all others the Range of Light, the most divinely beautiful of all the mountain chains I have seen.

—*John Muir*

This book is dedicated to my son Jacobus,
who suggested we do this trip
and who was such a wonderful companion on it,
and to the Sierra Club,
which has worked relentlessly
since the days of John Muir,
its first president,
to protect the Sierra Nevada
and wildlands throughout the world.

Contents

Introduction

The Sierra Nevada is one of the most beautiful mountain ranges in the world, and the John Muir Trail (JMT) winds through the very best of it. Hiking the JMT takes you through deep forests, along streams that cascade over smooth granite into quiet green pools of water begging to be swum in, past waterfalls and crystal blue lakes set in alpine basins, across flower-covered meadows that could be captured fairly only by a great impressionist painter, and over some of the highest mountain passes to be found in America. All of the trail is framed by 12,000-foot to 14,000-foot peaks with dramatic faces of granite, and which begins or ends, depending on whether you hike south to north or north to south, on Mt. Whitney, at 14,494 feet the highest mountain in the continental United States. It is a trail that is not interrupted by a road for 220 miles. If you want to hike 100 miles farther south, you can do it, again without crossing any roads. The trail is also blessed with the sunniest, warmest, most benign weather of any mountain range in the world.

I had wanted to hike the JMT since I was a Boy Scout growing up in Southern California. I continued to do a lot of backpacking into my twenties, but the introduction of

1

three kids and a demanding career took me away from backpacking for more than 20 years. It wasn't until Christmas 1994 that the idea of hiking the JMT became real. I had just decided to retire from my career as a civil rights attorney when my youngest son, Jacobus, then 19, handed me a Christmas card. It read, "You are invited to hike the John Muir Trail next summer with Leon and me." I was profoundly moved that my son would want to spend a month in the wilderness with his brother and me and instantly said, "What a great idea. Let's do it."

But the summer of 1995 did not work out for us. The preceding winter saw the Sierras receive the second-largest snowfall in 100 years; in late July, the passes were still covered in heavy snow and the high passes, such as Forester Pass (13,200 feet) had snow extending six to eight miles on each side. Most of the snow on the passes had partially melted, forming giant snow cups six feet across. Hiking over these snow cups would have been extremely slow and difficult and getting over the passes themselves would have required advanced snow and ice techniques. Even more dangerous than the passes would be fording many of the side streams, which, swelled by the heavy snow runoff, would have required hiking up to five to six miles upstream to find safe crossings. Hiking five to six miles upstream to cross a stream, of course, meant hiking five to six miles more to return to the JMT, all cross-country—a total of 10 to 12 miles, which is a day's worth of hiking just to cross one stream. The Tuolumne Meadows ranger I spoke with predicted, "No one will hike the JMT this year." Whether or not his prediction proved accurate, I know the conditions deterred us.

Many events intervened in our lives over the course of the next few years, and the JMT trip seemed to recede into the background. But in June 2000, Jacobus handed me a blues CD, along with a birthday/Father's Day note (I was born on Father's Day). The note read, "I've been rethinking how much I'd love to do the John Muir Trail with you (and Leon, if he's available) sometime before you're 60. Maybe summer or early fall of 2001?" I guess he thought my arms or legs might fall off when I turned 60. In any case, his proposal was received with great enthusiasm, and Jacobus, Leon and I decided we'd do it in 2001. When Jacobus got a job in 2001 as an environmental educator and trip leader, a job that continued through the end of August, we decided to start the hike the first week in September. This was more than fine with me, as September has long been my favorite month for hiking in the Sierras.

This book is a story of that hike, but it also is a guide for preparing for and planning to do such a trip in the easiest way possible. Long hikes with heavy packs are not particularly difficult for young backpackers. When I was in my 20s, my wife and I spent three months doing week-long backpacking trips in the Rockies and I was able to carry 50- to 60-pound packs without expiring; I once even carried a 68-pound pack on a 75-mile loop in the Sierras. But the days of carrying heavy packs had long passed me by and the question I faced was whether an underfit 58-year-old retired lawyer with more sports injuries than he wants to acknowledge could get in good-enough shape to not only survive hiking the JMT, but to hike it comfortably and enjoy every day. In the pages that follow, I explain how I did it, how anyone willing to follow some simple, commonsense guidelines can do it, and what an amazing experience hiking this incredible trail is. Indeed, it is an experience I hope all of you will share someday.

Preparing to Hike
the John Muir Trail

What's the Best Time to Go?

The JMT has been traveled at all times of the year, even winter, when it can be skied and snowshoed. But the most common time for hiking the trail is summer and fall. Most of the JMT is above 9,000 feet, so snow can be a factor, even then. In a normal year, snow will clear from the high passes by mid-July and not begin until early November, although some snow may fall as early as Labor Day. In dry years, it may be possible to begin hiking in early June; in wet years, it's prudent to wait until August. Know that there have been some years—like the historic 1995 snowfall, when snow remained on all the passes and much of the JMT throughout the summer. The first time I climbed Mt. Whitney, it snowed on the summit. I have a great photo of myself holding my four-month-old son, Leon, both of us bundled up in winter gear—and this was in the middle of July! So, traveling in the Sierras, like traveling anywhere at high elevations, can include some unpredictable weather. Summer and early-fall snowfalls tend to be one-day affairs and normally do not inhibit hiking. Nevertheless, rogue storms in September and October are possible and anyone traveling in the fall must be prepared.

The winter snowpack varies each year, so be sure to determine conditions before embarking. This is particularly important for getting over some of the high passes, as in high snowpack years it might be necessary to travel in snow even in late July or August, and perhaps an ice-ax and/or crampons will be needed for climbing and descending the high passes. Determining snow conditions is a simple task. The rangers at Yosemite National Park and Sequoia/Kings Canyon National Parks monitor snow conditions on a weekly basis and are prepared to answer questions by phone about trail conditions. Yosemite, Kings Canyon and Sequoia NPs (National Parks) also have websites, with updates. Yosemite NP can be reached at 559/372-0200, or http://www.nps.gov/yose; Kings Canyon/Sequoia NP is at http://www.nps.gov/seki. The Great Outdoors Recreation Pages (GORP) have a lot of general information, including some trail conditions, and are reached at http://www.gorp.com.

Weather aside, there are other reasons to hike the JMT in summer. Many plans are determined by school and vacation schedules. The sun comes up earlier in the morning during the summer, it is warmer during the day, and the mountain streams and lakes are very inviting when it's hot. The nights also are warmer and the days longer, which is a big advantage. But there are disadvantages to hiking in the summer, as well. There are far more people on the trail, including day-hikers and people taking shorter backpacking trips, as well as the JMT hikers (known on the trail as "through hikers"). This means there will be more people competing for the same wonderful campsite, you may have to share that exquisite swimming hole you chance upon, and you may even hear unwanted noise from an adjacent campsite when you would prefer complete wilderness silence. These are not horrible problems, as most of the people you meet on the trail are nice. Sometimes it is great to share a campfire with people you meet along the trail—indeed, fine friendships have begun this way—and maybe you don't want perfect silence, anyway. It is never too crowded on the JMT to have a great time, and, unlike the Appalachian Trail, where hikers are expected to camp in cramped, rat-infested wooden shacks established at regular intervals, it is almost always possible to get away from others and find a private campsite.

A more serious early-summer concern can be some of the stream crossings. Particularly after heavy snowfall years, some of the streams in early summer can be quite high, and even dangerous, if not forded with care. In some cases, high streams could force you to hike up the stream toward its headwaters to locate a safe spot to cross. This could be an enjoyable side trip and an exhilarating challenge, or an unwanted delay. In either case, it will make the JMT longer in both time and miles.

My preference is hiking in September and October, which have long been my favorite months for many outdoor adventures. While it is colder in the fall, the days shorter and the nights longer, it is not too cold for comfort and there still is enough daylight for a productive hiking day, a leisurely dinner and a fine sunset. Hiking weather in the fall can be perfect; normally, in September and early October you will be hiking with temperatures in the mid-60s to mid-70s. Going uphill with a pack on your back, you may be glad it's not in the mid-80s. You will build up plenty of heat and sweat in the 65-75 degree temperature range to want to jump into a nearby stream or lake, no matter how cold (and, by the way, the streams and lakes will be warmer in the fall than during summer), and the sun will be plenty hot when you get out to spend time catching rays on a smooth slab of granite.

The stream crossings in the fall will present no danger, as they might earlier in the hiking season. Yet, there will never be a problem of too little water. We hiked the JMT during what was considered a relatively "dry" year, yet water was abundant—so abundant, that by the middle of the trip, in order to save a little weight, we weren't even filling our water containers, knowing that wherever we ran out there would be a stream or lake nearby. There also will be far fewer people in the backcountry in the fall. I've been hiking in the Sierras during the fall for nearly 30 years and it seems like Labor Day weekend is almost a demarcation line between summer crowds and fall solitude. Dave Gordon, the backcountry ranger in Evolution Basin, one of the most beautiful and popular areas along the JMT, told me that he sees 50 to 60 backpackers on a typical day in mid-August, but in September he sees five to six backpackers a day.

Lastly, and this is a biggie for me—*there are no bugs in the fall!* I know the damn mosquitoes are part of wilderness, but I don't like them no matter how natural they are.

North to South or South to North?

Some might consider this issue a classic example of "six one-way, a half-dozen the other," but I think there are real differences. Hiking south to north requires starting at

Whitney Portal, where backpacking permits are hard to get because so many people depart at that trailhead just to hike Mt. Whitney. It requires a straight uphill climb of more than 6,000 feet over the course of 10.2 miles—8.0 miles of which you will be walking with a full pack—followed two days later by a climb over Forester Pass (13,200 feet), which generally is considered the toughest pass on the JMT. This would be at a time, of course, when you are probably in the worst physical shape you will be on during your JMT hike, when you are least acclimated to the elevation, and when you will be carrying perhaps your heaviest load, as the first realistic resupply spot will not be reached for six to seven days, or more. I just wonder how many prospective JMT hikers have turned back at this point, screaming, "I don't want any more of this!" But, if this is your idea of fun, or you crave unnecessary pain and challenge, start in the south.

Even though you ultimately will be hiking the same number of miles and climbing slightly more elevation, the easier route starts in the north, either in Yosemite Valley, or in Tuolumne Meadows. Starting in Yosemite Valley requires ascending nearly 6,000 feet, but the ascent is spread out over 16½ miles (from the valley to the top of Cathedral Pass) and only two to three days of supplies need be carried as there is an easy resupply spot at the Tuolumne Meadows Store. Starting at any of the alternative trailheads in Tuolumne Meadows permits an easy acclimation hike up gradual Lyell Canyon, followed by a relatively easy climb of Donohue Pass. Furthermore, the passes throughout the northern section of the JMT are lower and less rigorous than the higher passes in the southern section. Hiking north to south, you climb the toughest passes (Glen, Forester, Whitney) when you are stronger. Doesn't that make sense?

Lastly, although one guidebook describes the south to north route as "the classic trip," the fact is that when John Muir first hiked the crest of the Sierras, he hiked it north to south. Be like John, hike his trail north to south and you will be a happier camper.

Hiking the JMT in Sections

Most people who hike the JMT do it in one hike, but there is no law that says you have to. If the only way you can do it is in sections, then do it in sections. Read "Resupply Options" if you decide to go this route.

Having taken many one-week backpacking trips in my life, but only one month-long wilderness trip, I want to add one important comment. Taking a month or so to hike the JMT is not just a longer trip, it is a qualitatively different trip. As I hope my journal of the actual hike conveys, the experience of being in wilderness deepens exponentially as the time spent there increases. It almost takes a week for the effects of normal life patterns to break down, or wear off, and the flow of nature to take over. I know that the feelings and experiences I had during the last two weeks of our hike were qualitatively different than the feelings and experiences of the first week. By the end of the trip, I had lost contact with, or any sense of need for, my earthly possessions and normal routines and had given myself completely to the healing power and spirituality of wilderness. No weeklong trip I've ever taken, even trips to indescribably beautiful places, matches this.

How Long Should I Take? How Fast Should I Hike?

The length of time people we either met or heard about were taking from one week to 45 days to hike the JMT. So, the short answer to the question is, "The time it takes to hike the JMT can be anything you want it to be, or have the strength and/or time for."

While Jacobus and I were hiking the JMT, we heard about a German who was attempting to set a Guinness Book record by hiking the JMT both ways in just two weeks—i.e., approximately 32 miles a day. We didn't actually meet him (he probably passed us by in the middle of the night), but we spoke with many JMT hikers about him. Absolutely no one we spoke with understood why anyone would want to do such a trip, other than just to get a name in a record book, because you can't hike at that pace and enjoy what you are doing. He was hiking so fast, we were told, that to conserve weight he didn't even carry a sleeping bag. Also, he didn't want to take the time taking clothes off to get into his bag or to put them back on in the morning. We also ran into a hiker, "The Purple Hat Man," who had hiked the JMT twice—once in 45 days and a second time in 13 days. He told us he much preferred the long hike as it gave him time to fish, swim, take days off for side hikes, and just relax. Hiking the JMT in 13 days, he said, was, "All hiking, there is no time for anything else."

Most of the hikers we met were hiking 10 to 13 miles per day and doing the JMT in three weeks. When we said we were hiking eight to 10 miles a day and taking a month, many said to us, "Gee, I wish I had that much time." Many had to fit the trip into three-week vacations; many had responsibilities to wives and families that couldn't be shunted for a month; some, particularly the young stallions hiking alone, simply wanted to hike faster and had the youth, testosterone, and strength to do so.

Perhaps John Muir most perfectly captured the issue of time when he wrote,

> "Another glorious Sierra day in which one seems to be dissolved and absorbed and sent pulsing onward we know not where. Life seems neither long nor short, and we take no more heed to save time or make haste than do the trees and stars. This is true freedom, a good practical sort of immortality."

If I were to do it again, I would want to take more time, not less. I would want to live the Muir ideal and make sure there was extra time to take more side hikes and have more layover days. I would swim in all the marvelous streams and lakes we passed and leave more time to just sit quietly in one spot and contemplate everything around me. However, not everyone has the luxury of that much time. A great trip can be had in three weeks, but an even better trip is awaiting those with four weeks, or more.

Is the Hike Dangerous? Should I Fear the Heights?

As I was writing this book, I happened to run into Oakland, California, Mayor Jerry Brown at an athletic club in downtown Oakland, and mentioned that I had just hiked the JMT. The first thing he asked was, "Did you carry a gun?" I said, "Why would I carry a gun?" "To protect yourself from wild animals," Jerry replied. I explained that the Sierras were not Africa (or even downtown

Oakland) and that animals present little or no danger on the JMT to anyone who is prepared and acts responsibly. Driving to the trailhead is more dangerous than the occasional bear you might encounter or the mountain lions that exist in isolated places but are rarely ever seen by humans. Guns are not required, and who would want to carry the extra weight, anyway?

Bears are a danger to food, but almost never to humans—unless you get between a mother bear and her cubs, or are dumb enough to try to take stolen food away from a bear—which I once tried to do to a Yosemite bear when I was young, foolish, and invulnerable. Probably the most serious danger would be encountered crossing swollen streams or descending an icy snowbank on a high pass in early summer. Carrying food in bear canisters (which is required in the national parks) and avoiding high water and late snow eliminates all these potential dangers.

The JMT itself is in great shape, and, for the most part, is well-contoured and well-marked. And, since you are almost always walking north-south, or south-north, along the Sierra Nevada crest, it's almost impossible to get lost. Even if you did manage to do so, there are enough people hiking to steer you back in the right direction.

As for fear of heights, I am not an expert on acrophobia (actually, I'm not an expert on anything), but the JMT is well-traveled by both stock and people and generally is quite wide, as trails go. There are a few spots near the tops of passes that have a long way down, but you would almost have to jump over the edge to actually fall. The only spot in the whole trail that gave me any pause was the east side of the top of Trail Crest coming down from our hike to the top of Whitney, and the only reason that part concerned me was that we were hiking it at night with weak flashlight batteries and I was hobbling on seven blisters. Hiking that same section in the light of day would have caused me no worry at all.

Backcountry Rangers

You are not alone on the JMT. In addition to other hikers, there are summer backcountry rangers stationed in Yosemite at Little Yosemite Valley, in Tuolumne Meadows (Visitor Center), in the John Muir Wilderness at Purple Lake, and in Sequoia and Kings Canyon National Parks at McClure Meadow, Le Conte Canyon, Rae Lakes, Charlotte Lake, and Crabtree Meadow. These rangers are stationed in the backcountry from early summer to at least Labor Day, and some stay in the backcountry until mid-October. They don't just sit in their cabins, but often are out hiking the trails in their areas. Thus, if you go to a ranger cabin and find the ranger out, she/he may be away for days and you might have to solve your problem yourself. On the other hand, the ranger may be nearby; in all cases, leave a note. The rangers carry short-wave radio phones and can call other rangers to look for that missing hiker or determine trail conditions up ahead. They can also call out for help in an emergency.

The backcountry rangers serve the dual function of assisting hikers and enforcing rules, such as bear canister requirements and limitations on open fires above certain designated elevations. They generally are extremely nice people and many have become hugely knowledgeable about the Sierras in general and their areas in particular. Many of the rangers have been stationed in their areas for more than one season, and some have been stationed in the same or adjacent areas for as many as 25 seasons. They are true lovers and protectors of the wilderness.

Resupply Options

Unless you are a crazy German trying to hike the JMT in a week, you will need to be resupplied somewhere along the trail. Without resupplying, if you are taking the normal three to four weeks to hike the trail, you would have to carry an 80- to 90-pound pack, which few people want to do (we did meet two guys from Oklahoma who were doing exactly that). The simplest and most effective way of lightening your load on the JMT is to be resupplied as often as possible. You also should consider mailing back the garbage you have been carrying and any equipment that you have taken but are not using. Since there are many things you should not burn or dump in the wilderness (like excess food, packaging for freeze-dried food, plastic, and toilet paper), mailing these things back to your home in the same container your resupplies arrived in saves you the weight (and space in your pack) of carrying unwanted items to the end of the JMT. To do this, you will need to include in your resupply boxes a pre-paid UPS or Federal Express shipping label. If you want to make the hiking as easy and pleasurable as possible, I have a few more resupply tips for you.

First, there are some very easy resupply spots you can take advantage of. The Tuolumne Meadows Store, which you reach around mile 24 if you start in Yosemite Valley, is almost right on top of the JMT and the store will accept and hold mailed packages of supplies for backpackers. Mail address for re-supplies is the Tuolumne Meadows Store, c/o General Delivery, Tuolumne Meadows, CA

95389 (209/372-8421). The store carries a decent supply of food for sale, including cold beer. After leaving the store don't try to cross Highway 120 because you'd be going the wrong way. Stay on the south side of the highway and continue east a few hundred yards to the Tuolumne Meadows Campground, where you will reconnect with the JMT. The store and campground both have public phones, which you will share with 1,000 other campers and visitors to Tuolumne Meadows; if you have the patience to wait, you can phone home, perhaps to discover your lover has fallen in love with someone else, then return to the JMT with a broken heart. But, after just a few miles on the trail, absorbing the beauty of magnificent Lyell Canyon, you will realize that your lover didn't deserve you anyway, that being on the JMT is much healthier and more exciting than living in the city with an ingrate, and you will proceed to have the great trip you deserve, relieved to know you won't have to return home to the wrong person. The JMT will have the same impact on any other personal problems you may have.

The second easy resupply spot is at the Reds Meadow Resort, which is approximately 36 miles south on the JMT from Tuolumne Meadows. The resort is just off the JMT and they accept and store mailed packages for backpackers at their store. The mail address for Reds Meadow Resort is P.O. Box 395, Mammoth Lakes, CA 93546 (760/934-2345). Reds Meadow Resort is kind of a grubby place but it is shown on the topographical map you will be carrying and thus is very easy to find. Cross the steel bridge over the Middle Fork of the San Joaquin River, turn right toward Devils Postpile and walk about ½ mile through the Postpile to a fork in the trail; take the left fork, walk another ½ mile, and you will reach a road which is at the entrance to Reds Meadow Resort. Follow this road to the right and it will lead you to the resort in a quarter-mile or so. At the resort, you will find a store with some basic supplies, a café and a few cabins (if you desperately need a bad meal, hot shower, or night in a sagging bed). If your equipment needs are more serious, you have the option of catching a seasonal shuttle bus (for a fee) to Mammoth Lakes, about 20 minutes away by shuttle, or using one of the two pay phones to call a private shuttle service to pick you up (they are listed in the yellow pages). Or you might call your stockbroker, only to learn that he's the person your lover ran off with and that the value of your portfolio has dropped 20 percent in the past week.

Seriously, Mammoth is a large ski resort and is full of outdoor supply stores; if you can't find what you need there, it probably doesn't exist. Mammoth is the last place near the JMT where you will be able to find equipment you might need and couldn't find at either the Tuolumne Meadows Store or the Reds Meadow Store. Mammoth also is noteworthy for its schlocky, overbuilt, and badly designed architecture—the type that never should be permitted in beautiful places—so you will be relieved to leave the place and return to the JMT.

Once on the JMT again, you will want to hike to either the Lake Edison Trail (approximately 32 miles from Reds Meadow Resort), where you will have to detour west to the Vermillion Valley Resort at the far west end of Lake Edison, or to the Muir Trail Ranch (approximately 20 miles south of the Lake Edison Trail, for your next resupply. Of the two, the Muir Trail Ranch is the better choice; it is just one mile off the JMT, whereas getting to the Vermillion Valley Resort requires either a long boat ride (fee required) across Lake Edison on a ferry that only operates twice a day, and you probably won't know when, or hiking 6.2 miles there and 6.2 miles back—in other words, a full day of hiking just for supplies. Many people do this, however, as the Vermillion Valley Resort charges $25 to hold supplies for hikers and the Muir Trail Ranch charges $45, the difference apparently based on the fact that the Muir Trail Ranch people (instead of you!) carry in the mailed supplies by horseback from the road-end at the west side of Florence Lake (the same name as my dear mother). I don't know about you, but my days are worth more than $20. I'd rather use that day swimming in a mountain stream, skipping smooth rocks in a lake, reading a book, taking an extra layover day or, if I'm going to hike that day, continue down the JMT, and not hike a side trail that traverses a dam-controlled lake that is often little more than mud by midsummer. You pay your money and you make your choices and in this case the easy choice is Muir Trail Ranch. If you decide to camp nearby while you sort out your resupplies, there is a wonderful hot springs just across the South Fork of the San Joaquin River from Muir Trail Ranch and campsites on both sides of the river.

To reach the Muir Trail Ranch from the north, on the descent from Senger Creek take a lateral to the right which is shown on the map for .9 mile to the Florence Lake Trail heading west; the Ranch is about .25 mile further west. Hiking from the south, 1.8 miles past the junction with the Piute Pass Trail take the Florence Lake Trail west about 1.7 miles to Muir Trail Ranch. To reach the Vermillion Valley Resort, take the Lake Edison Trail

southwest 2.0 miles to a junction with the short trail leading to a ferry landing for the twice-daily ferry ride across
Lake Edison to the Vermillion Valley Resort, or hike 4.2
miles on the north side of Lake Edison to the Resort.

You get your supplies to the Vermillion Valley Resort
by mailing them to P.O. Box 258, Lakeshore, CA 93634
(209/259-4000), and to Muir Trail Ranch by mailing
them to Box 176, Lakeshore, CA 93634 (autumn/winter
phone: 209/966-3195).

There are many side trails where supplies could be
obtained but none are short or easy; all require two to three
days of side hiking. See *Starr's Guide to the John Muir Trail
and the High Sierra Region,* Sierra Club Books, for details
and routes of side trails. To save time and labor, I recommend
arranging for a horse packer to resupply you for the southern half of the JMT. Since the stretch from Muir Trail Ranch
to Whitney Portal is approximately 120 miles, you will need
at least one and possibly two resupplies. We chose to be resupplied by horses twice—at Grouse Meadow and Rae
Lakes. By doing this, we carried just four to seven days of
food on each of three sections, not the eight to nine days of
food that would have been required if we had been resupplied only once. But we were averaging just eight miles per
day (including layover days); if you travel faster, one resupply will work fine. A resupply will cost approximately $400
for the two days it takes the packer to get in and out (the cost
of one night in a four-star hotel). This is more than some
backpackers will want to pay, but considered on a per-night
basis over the length of the trip it is not much for the greatest vacation you will ever have. You need to meet the packer
at a predetermined time and place so using a horse packer
can limit your spontaneity and flexibility, but if you get

resupplied within Sequoia or Kings Canyon National Parks you can ask the packer to leave your food in a bear box in case you are late arriving at your meeting place. If you want to be super-certain of not missing connections, you could ask the packer to wait an extra day for you in case you are late, but this will cost you an extra day's wages for the packer.

Many horse packers are available for hire. My favorite is Rainbow Pack Outfitters, 5845 South Lake Road, Bishop, CA 93514 (760/873-8877).

Pets

Pets, other than horses, of course, are not permitted on trails in national parks. Since more than half of the JMT is in Yosemite, Kings Canyon and Sequoia National Parks, it would be a mistake to try to bring any pet larger than a tick with you.

Wilderness Permits

Permits are required in all wilderness areas and all backcountry in the national parks. They are the biggest bargains on the planet ($3 per person for the whole trip) but you need to apply for them well in advance of your hike if you will be leaving from any of the more popular trailheads, because your request for a permit is not considered separately from other requests to depart on the same trailhead that day, regardless of destination. In other words, the wilderness permit operates as a quota system just for the number of people leaving a particular trailhead on a particular day. It does not account for how long hikers will be in the backcountry or where they will be staying. The backpacker starting at Tuolumne Meadows intending to hike the JMT is treated exactly like a backpacker departing that same trailhead intending to camp in Lyell Canyon for one night. The system doesn't make complete sense, but it offers the advantage to the JMT hiker of not having to get a permit for designated campsites for every night, as well as not being locked into a rigid schedule of campsites, as is required in some national parks (such as Rocky Mountain National Park). So, freelance and extemporize to your heart's content.

If you will be starting from a Yosemite trailhead, permits can be reserved 24 weeks in advance of your start date by writing or calling Wilderness Reservations, P.O. Box 545, Yosemite, CA 05389 (559/372-0740). If beginning at Whitney Portal, you need to get a permit from the Inyo National Forest Wilderness Reservation System at P.O. Box 430, Big Pine, CA 93513 (888/374-3773). For starts from a trailhead in Kings Canyon or Sequoia National Parks, you can write or call Sequoia and Kings Canyon National Parks, Three Rivers, CA 93271 (209/565-3708). Permits in Kings Canyon and Sequoia National Parks are free, which is an even better bargain than the $3 fee in Yosemite NP. The wilderness reservation people, at least at Yosemite, are especially helpful to hikers planning to hike the complete JMT. It is still good advice to get your permit early, as I did in 2001, phoning Yosemite at 8 a.m., exactly 24 weeks in advance of your start date. But if for some reason you have to reschedule a start date, as I did in 1995 due to heavy snow conditions (which ultimately aborted our trip), mention you are a JMT hiker, and they will bust their buns to get you on the trail on the date you want, sometimes using an alternative trailhead not far from the one desired, or maybe just give you a permit for the time and place you want. Note, permits are easy to obtain for hikes in September and October; July and August are the busy months.

After you have gone through the trouble of reserving your permit, don't forget to pick it up. They must be picked up by 10 a.m. the day you start; if you are going to be late picking it up, call the permit office by 10 a.m. and ask them to hold the permit until you arrive. Otherwise, they may release your permit to other hikers.

You also will need a Mt. Whitney Zone Stamp, no matter where you start, if your JMT hike will take you into the Whitney area, which it definitely will if you are doing the full monty. This stamp costs $1, which should be included in the payment for the permit. You also should specify when you will be in the Mt. Whitney zone (which starts near Crabtree Ranger Station on the west and Outpost Camp on the east).

Physical Conditioning

If you are 100 pounds overweight and haven't exercised in years, you are going to need a lot of physical work before you hit the JMT. If you are young, strong, and fit and have been doing a lot of backpacking recently, you will need no pretrip conditioning. If you are older, you will need more preparation than if you are young. But, having led youth groups on hikes, I know firsthand that one can never assume the young always are in condition. Due to cutbacks in physical education programs in public schools, plus the prevalence of unhealthy fast-food diets, the number of overweight and obese young people has exploded in the last ten years. A 2001 study of junior high and high school students found that 77 percent of California students failed to meet minimum standards of physical fitness. But even out-of-condition young people have the capacity to get in shape relatively quickly on the trail; they may whine and complain for a few days, but by the fourth day, they are in better physical condition and they're going to be OK. Middle-aged backpackers who are not already in shape will require more discipline and preparation.

One theory of backpacking is that you get in shape as you go. That theory can work some of the time, but it almost always comes at a heavy price—usually a miserable first week, blisters on soft feet, and/or back or hip problems caused by lack of practice carrying a heavy backpack. I don't recommend pursuing this theory.

Before our JMT hike, Jacobus and I were representative of two types of people who hike the JMT. Jacobus had been working with high school kids all summer doing three-week backpack trips in the backcountry of Washington. That was great preparation. When he first lifted his 54-pound pack, he said, "This is light," and proceeded to take even more weight as the trip progressed, never showing evidence of fatigue or pain.

My situation was more typical of the type of person I hope to encourage to take such trips. I was 58 years old when I hiked the JMT, moderately fit, but also deskbound in both my profession and lifestyle. My normal physical exercise routine consisted of some half-court basketball about twice a week—a game described most charitably as a "slow white game" or, as someone once described us, "Wannabees who never were"—plus an occasional bike ride of about 15 miles over hilly terrain, 10–15 minutes of weightlifting two to three times a week, plus rigorous sex at least 47 times a week (don't I wish!). I backpacked once or twice a year, generally nothing long or hard. I hiked occasionally in the local parks and the Sierras and cross-country skied occasionally in the winter. In short, I wasn't exactly a marathoner or triathlete and my routine was pretty moderate.

I decided early on that I didn't want to just survive the JMT, I wanted to hike it comfortably so I could enjoy every day. Therefore, to get in shape I increased my exercise moderately and focused my exercise more on my legs. In 1998, I had prepared for a trek in Nepal with my son Leon by cycling three to four times a week, and had found when I had to face some of the steep climbs I was in excellent shape. My Sherpas complimented me to other people by saying, "He walks Sherpa speed," which meant I kept up with them. Of course, they were carrying 60–70 pound loads and I was carrying a 10–15 pound day-pack, including my camera equipment. This experience taught me two things: (1) The Sherpa people are incredibly generous; and (2) Cycling is great conditioning for hiking. With this in mind, beginning about eight weeks before the start of our JMT hike I hiked or cycled three to four times a week, with a little basketball thrown in on the other days.

Of course, I am fortunate to have a regional park five minutes from my house that is hilly and quite beautiful. It provided both hiking and cycling opportunities for me to prepare for the JMT.

My road cycling route was 15 miles long, with three climbs and a total of 1,350-foot elevation gain. I never pushed myself, as I usually rode with a friend and we would talk throughout the ride, but I noticed that our time for completing the route decreased somewhat to about an hour and a quarter, and my legs felt much stronger at the end of my eight weeks of preparation. That last hill, which previously had seemed long to me, became just a blip on the radar screen.

For my hiking, I picked a particularly beautiful 2.2-mile hike with steep ups-and-downs; I estimate it at about 800 feet of total elevation gain and loss. When I began doing this hike, I would get winded on the steep uphill sections, sometimes even having to stop for a drink or to catch my breath, and it took me about an hour and a quarter to finish. As time went on, I didn't have to stop or slow down on the uphill sections and I was finishing the hike in less time. By the week before we were to start the JMT, I was hiking uphill as fast as I could walk on the level sections and completing the hike in 45 minutes with less effort. While this was very encouraging, I kept telling myself I should be carrying a backpack to increase my conditioning, but I guess I was just too lazy to do that. As it turned out, this was a mistake. Although my legs were in pretty good shape by the time I began the JMT, my lack of practice carrying a backpack failed to prepare me for the weight that would be placed on my hips by the pack's hip-belt, and failed to alert me to the fact that my back-pack was not adjusted properly. Don't be as lazy and dumb as I was. Carry a loaded pack during your prepara-tion at least a few times.

My error of omission aside, I think it is clear that I didn't have to do a great amount of work to get ready to hike the JMT. Indeed, I just modestly increased the amount of exercise I was already doing and focused more on strengthening my legs. Probably many who read this book already have a more rigorous exercise routine than mine. But even for people starting from scratch, the amount of preparation needed to hike the JMT is not beyond the reach of anyone who is reasonably healthy and motivated. Know you can do it!

Taking Care of Feet

In anticipation of hiking the JMT, my biggest concern was not general fitness but the fitness of my feet. I was born with long, skinny feet, which matured to size 11AA, and I have had chronic problems finding shoes that fit, particularly hiking boots that didn't give me blisters. Would they develop blisters on top of blisters and make my hiking painful and/or unsuccessful? So for the first time in my life, I tried to learn as much as I could about foot care.

The first thing I began to do was to experiment with different boots and different types of boots, ranging from heavy mountaineering boots to lightweight running shoes. I will discuss boot selection more in the section on equipment that follows, but suffice it to say here that the heavier and more rigid the boots, the greater the chances they will be hard on your feet. Conversely, the lighter, softer and more flexible the boots, the more comfortable they are likely to be. If comfort was the only criterion, we'd probably all just hike in lightweight running shoes. However, you also must take into consideration the stiffness of the sole, as your feet will be landing on countless sharp rocks during the course of a long hike, the height and stiffness of the boot, as turning an ankle is always a possibility when walking on uneven surfaces, and water-proofing. If you have a trusty, comfortable pair of boots that you've been wearing for years and they are well-suited for hiking with a backpack, you have solved one part of the equation. If you buy a new pair of boots, you need to break them in before the hike. In either case, you still need to get your feet in shape.

To prepare my feet and then take care of them on the trail, I did a variety of things. First, I found and read *Fixing Your Feet: Prevention and Treatments for Athletes* by Jon Vonhof. The book was written primarily for ultra-marathoners, triathletes and long-distance hikers. It has more information about foot preparation and care than you ever thought existed and more than a 58-year-old brain was able to absorb and remember, but the parts I used really made a difference.

I bought and tried some foot products recommended by the book. First, I tried "Tuf-Foot," a product described as useful "on all domestic animals and humans" in "protecting feet against bruises, blisters, and foot soreness" by toughening the skin. It is a thin brown liquid that I spread on my heels and tops of my toes each night for about a month, then allowed to dry before going to bed. I did not take it on the JMT primarily because I didn't want to carry the bottle. It takes only 30 seconds to apply, dries quickly, has no noxious odors and did not stain anything. Although it claims to toughen skin, I did not notice that my skin was getting tougher. Nevertheless, in a month of hiking, I did not get a single blister on any of the places I had prepared with Tuf-Foot; the only blisters I got on the trail were on the bottom of my toes, an area I had failed to put Tuf-Foot on. My conclusion? This stuff works. Tuf-Foot can be ordered by phone (toll-free) 888/883-3668, by email at Tuffoot730@aol.com, by website at www.Tuf-Foot.com and by mail at Bonaseptic Co., The Roberts Building, Suite 107, 2996 Grandview Ave., N.E., Atlanta, GA 30305. And, if you don't use the stuff yourself, perhaps your dog or horse will like it.

I also bought and tested two products, "Bodyglide" and "Sportslick," that operate on the principle that by making the skin slippery where it tends to rub against the boot, friction is reduced and blisters are prevented. I think both products work, but in the places where I knew friction would be a problem, I used Dr. Scholl's Moleskin Plus and Dr. Scholl's Cushlin Blister Treatment. I have been using moleskin for 30 years but I found the new product, Cushlin Blister Treatment, to be superior. Moleskin works but it tends to peel off during the day as feet get hot and sweaty. Also, if you like to swim in streams and lakes, moleskin needs to be replaced after each swim since it is made of a padding that absorbs water—the enemy of healthy, unblistered feet.

The Cushlin Blister Treatment is more appropriately used to prevent blisters in the same way moleskin is used. The Blister Treatment basically consists of rubberized pads with a strong adhesive on the back, which you put on your feet where you expect blisters to develop. The pads do not absorb water, so you can swim with them on and not have to replace them—and they last for days. The only downside I see is that the adhesive is so strong, if you tried to take the pads off too soon they might take some skin along. The product brochure recommends soaking feet in warm water for 15 minutes before removing the pads. I never had to do this, as I just left them on until they began to peel off at the edges, generally after two to four days, and then they came off easily.

The other important tip I picked up from the book was its recommendation to wear gaiters at all times, which I did (Jacobus had been doing this for years). Gaiters prevent sand and pebbles from entering boots, lodging in socks, and grinding away at the skin. My socks stayed cleaner and less abrasive. Hiking with gaiters will be a permanent feature of all my future backpacking trips.

The last important tip about foot care was given to me by Jacobus: Let your feet dry at night. Dampness softens skin, as anyone who has been in a pool or hot shower too long knows, and letting feet dry at night protects and toughens the skin for the next day. Jacobus advised, and I followed his tip, that I take a pair of Teva sandals as my camp shoes and an extra pair of lightweight socks as my camp socks. These camp socks, unlike my hiking socks, which got wet during the day, would be dry each afternoon or evening when we stopped hiking, and they breathed well, allowing my feet to dry and stay dry for 14 to 18 hours before I would next put on my hiking boots and heavy socks.

These simple foot care techniques greatly enhanced the health of my feet, and the pleasure of the hike.

Equipment and Food

Back in the 1950s, when I began backpacking as a Boy Scout, there was no such thing as lightweight backpacking gear, or at least no one I knew or ever met on a trail had any. I carried a 10-pound kapok-filled sleeping bag, a full-length, very heavy, canvas and rubber air mattress, a tent made out of heavy canvas smeared with some kind of green gunk allegedly to make it waterproof (it still leaked like a sieve), heavy hardwood tent poles and stakes, and canned goods. All of this was carried in a Yucca Pack, purchased for $5 from the Boy Scout catalogue. The pack was nothing more than a canvas sack with thin, canvas-webbed shoulder straps and no waistbelt. Down clothing? Gore-Tex waterproof shells? Forget it. We carried heavy, heat-inefficient, cotton, wool, and kapok-insulated clothing, and rain shells of heavy, nonbreathable, rubberized canvas. You would have thought we were hunters driving Jeeps on Forest Service roads into the backcountry to find prey, overeat, get drunk, brag about women, and generally make fools of ourselves. To compound the felony, we would secretly stuff rocks in some scouts' packs, which often did not get discovered until the end of the day when the pack was unloaded. I don't recall ever weighing any of the packs we carried, but they were damn heavy. I vividly remember some of the scouts crying and begging to go home, usually to be told they were wimps and sissies. "Shut up and hike, girls!" I have no idea how many thousands of dollars and thousands of hours were expended on psychotherapy as a result of these backpacking experiences, but I am sure the numbers are substantial. I'm only surprised that any of us continued backpacking. The lure of wilderness must be strong.

Today's hiker is the beneficiary of many revolutions in backpacking equipment and the equipment choices we now have simply would be unrecognizable to past generations of hikers. But while all choices are pretty good, some are better, and lighter, than others. I will try to navigate through some of these choices so that you can embark on the trail with the lightest feasible pack for you. Note, I say "lightest feasible pack for you," not "lightest pack." The difference is important. As you get closer and closer to the "lightest" pack, you give up comforts—the lightest tent, for example, could be very small, making sitting up, getting dressed inside, and keeping your pack in the tent and out of the rain, difficult, if not impossible. A heavier tent may be bigger and more comfortable to use, but you have the burden of carrying it all day. Some JMT hikers have even not brought sleeping bags, choosing to save weight by sleeping in all their clothes. That isn't a very attractive option for me, as I wouldn't want to take the chance of losing sleep or catching a cold, but not carrying a bag certainly saves weight. You may want to bring along a camera, a pair of binoculars, a deck of cards, a novel—all nice luxuries, but you pay the price in added weight. In the end, you will have to decide what you really need, and how to resolve the weight vs. comfort issues. In making these decisions, I suggest using a postage scale to weigh the items you are stuffing in your pack; Weight Watchers sells a wonderful little electronic scale that serves this purpose well. Weighing items not only will allow you to compare actual weights and make more intelligent choices, but also will increase your consciousness about the things going in your pack and cause you to ask, "Do I really need this? Or, "How often am I really going to use this?"

During the last few years, traditional notions of what to carry when backpacking have been challenged by the concept of ultralight backpacking, often referred to as lightpacking. *Backpacker* magazine calls the proponents Lightniks. In 2002, I hiked the 180-mile Tahoe-to-Yosemite Trail with my niece Unmi employing many lightpacking ideas and equipment. Since she weighs just 100 pounds and has a limited carrying capacity, utilizing lightpacking techniques was essential for the trip.

The difference in weight between what Unmi and I carried on the Tahoe-to-Yosemite Trail and what Jacobus and I carried on the JMT was amazing. Jacobus and I began the Tuolumne Meadows to Red Meadows section (six days) carrying a total of 104 pounds—57 for Jacobus and 47 on my back. Unmi and I began the first segment of the Tahoe-to-Yosemite Trail (four days) carrying just 62 pounds—25 for Unmi and 37 for me. Adding eight pounds of food for two days to make the comparison accurate, lightpacking concepts saved Unmi and me approximately 34 pounds of weight. When you plan to take 750,000 steps and climb 50,000 feet of elevation, 34 pounds between two people is a lot. Carrying 10 pounds less weight, I could cover more ground, climb more elevation, and not be as tired. And since I intend to continue taking long hikes, despite getting older, I anticipate a lot of lightpacking in my future. Unless you are a complete masochist, you should at least should consider the lightweight options.

The leading pioneer in lightpacking is Ray Jardine, who has published a fine and provocative book on the topic, *Beyond Backpacking: Ray Jardine's Guide to Lightweight Hiking,* AdventureLore Press (2001), www.Adventure Lore.com. Also worth noting is The *Ultralight Backpacker,* by Ryel Kestenbaum, Ragged Mountain Press/McGraw Hill (2001). While Jardine's book is the more comprehensive of the two, much of Jardine's equipment is self-made, so this may have a limited utility for those not willing to make their own clothes and equipment. Nevertheless, as time goes on, it is almost certain that many of Jardine's ideas will take hold and commercial lightweight products will emerge in response to consumer demand. Indeed, one such company, GoLite, already is in the market with revolutionary lightweight packs, tents, and sleeping bags, and Stephenson's Warmlite has been in the market making lightweight tents for many years.

The ultimate lightnik may have been John Muir, who carried no pack, no sleeping bag or pad, no tent, few clothes, and little of anything else. He would walk into the wilderness wearing a wool coat, with a hunk of shepherd's bread under his belt and a bag of tea and sugar in his pocket. At night, he slept next to a fire. When it rained and the wind blew, he would climb to the top of the highest tree and howl with the wind, exhilarated to be feeling the power of nature as the tree swayed and lightning flashed around him, undaunted by the rain or cold.

The rest of us carry gear.

Shelters

You have four choices: tarp, bivy sack, tent or nothing. The preferred choice is nothing, as nothing weighs nothing, nothing provides the best ventilation, and nothing maximizes your contact with nature more than having nothing between you and the sky. But part of nature is rain, wind, hail, snow, and bugs. You can eliminate bugs by hiking in the fall, but your chances of rain, wind, hail, and snow disappearing are small. Nature, although blessed, is a force to contend with, and is not predictable. We had 28 days of almost perfect weather on our JMT hike in September-October, but I spoke with someone who hiked the JMT in July, normally the best weather month, and he encountered seven straight days of rain during his hike. I've experienced snow in July in the Sierras. Consequently, nearly everyone who hikes the JMT will need some type of shelter.

Tarps are the lightest choice for a shelter. A tarp large enough for two persons (about 8 feet square) will weigh around 1½ pounds. The groundcover you will need to go with the tarp will weigh about ½ pound, a total of about two pounds for the simplest tarp system. There also are more sophisticated tarp systems, such as the Bibler Megamid, which uses an aluminum pole to hold up the middle, somewhat like a tepee, and weighs 3½ pounds, and the Black Diamond Beta Light, smaller than the Megamid, but weighing in at 1½ pounds. The advantage of a tarp is lightness and excellent ventilation (an advantage after a night of noxious odors emanating from your tent-mate following a bean dinner or the smell of sweaty bodies that haven't washed or swum for days), but there are disadvantages. The very ventilation that is so nice in moderate weather becomes a negative in cold weather. This could require you to carry a heavier sleeping bag, thereby losing some of the weight advantage of a tarp. A tarp will keep most of the rain or snow off you, but not all. Some amount invariably blows in with the wind or flows in via rivulets of water on the ground, particularly if you have pitched the tarp in the wrong spot or not trenched around the perimeter. Tarps also are much harder to put up properly as they are not freestanding and require support from all sides and sometimes from above.

There also are a few hybrids on the market—tarps that can be ordered with a tentlike structure made from thin nylon and/or mosquito netting that is hung, tentlike, under the tarp. GoLite (www.golite.com) has such a hybrid, which it calls the Lair Nest 1 (one-person), and Lair Nest 2 (two-person). But the small two-person, with tarp and stakes, weighs more than two pounds, roughly the same as the Warmlite 2R tent I describe below, and the Warmlite is much easier to set up, and is stronger and bigger. The Warmlite tents are far more expensive, however, than the GoLites ($499 compared to less than $100 for the GoLites). If you amortize the cost of equipment over its expected life, even an expensive tent is cheap on a per night basis, but if you don't have the cash, the GoLites may be the direction you want to go.

Bivy Sacks: A bivy sack essentially is a sleeping bag enclosure, with a small amount of headroom on one end. Some come with aluminum or fiberglass hoops to hold the sack over the head, some omit the extra weight of a hoop. They are big enough for one person and no gear. Bivy sacks solve some of the disadvantages of tarps, since they are full enclosures, but they add others, as your gear remains outside, subject to the elements. And bivy sacks are incredibly claustrophobic because they are so small. They are light, with most weighing around two pounds (for one person), but sleeping in a bivy sack is like sleeping in a coffin. If you are seeking a return to the womb, or a preview of the death experience, maybe the bivy sack is for you.

Tents: About 95 percent of the hikers we encountered on the JMT carried tents. But the similarities end there, as there is almost an infinite number and variety of tents on the market. There are three-season and four-season tents, one-wall and two-wall tents, freestanding and non-freestanding tents, and tents for one, two, three, or four persons.

Should you carry a three-season or four-season tent? The answer is simple: Unless you are trying to ski the JMT in the winter, forget the four-season tent. It is constructed for conditions you will never encounter, such as high winds and snow loads, and is overbuilt and too heavy for summer or fall use on the JMT.

Freestanding or non-freestanding? An advantage of a freestanding tent is that it can be pitched without using any tent stakes and generally is easier to pitch. Also, it can be pitched anywhere, or moved to a better spot just by picking it up. But freestanding tents rely on multiple tent poles for support and, thus, generally are heavier. Non-freestanding tents require more careful placement and the use of stakes, but they perform just as well as the freestanding tents (which usually should be staked anyway if there is any prospect of strong winds) and are slightly lighter.

One wall or two? Almost all good-quality backpacking tents are made with two walls. The reason is that one-wall tents are made with waterproof fabric that does not permit water vapor from breathing and sweating inside the tent to escape; thus, even in dry weather, condensation builds up inside the walls of the tent and you get wet. The two-wall tent solves this problem by making the outer wall (rain-fly) out of waterproof fabric, and the inner wall out of thin, breathable fabric, with a few inches in between the layers to allow air to flow. This separation is crucial, because if the outer waterproof wall falls onto the inner wall, you will have a one-wall tent that will not breathe. Consequently, it always is essential to tighten the tent before heading to bed to make sure your expensive two-wall tent has not become a one-wall tent.

Some tent manufacturers have tried to solve the rain/condensation problem by making one-wall tents out of expensive Gore-Tex, but this hasn't worked. Gore-Tex works fine in dry weather, as it permits condensation to escape through the material, but Gore-Tex doesn't breathe when it is wet. In a rainstorm, Gore-Tex functions like the cheapest, nonbreathable, one-wall tent you could buy at Wal-Mart, and you will suffer the effects of condensation until the tent fabric dries.

Two-person, two-wall backpacking tents generally weigh around five pounds and provide 30 to 35 square feet of floor space, including any vestibule for entry and storage of packs. Three-person tents generally weigh seven to eight pounds and provide 40 to 50 square feet of space.

For our JMT trip, Jacobus insisted on a three-person tent. Two years earlier, he had hiked 250 miles along the

Pacific Crest Trail in Washington with a friend, and they had appreciated the luxury of the space in a three-person tent. He and his friend were young and strong and the extra two to three pounds didn't faze them. I preferred carrying a lighter two-person tent, but I deferred to him on this issue. I had a three-person North Face tent weighing 7½ pounds, which had worked well in the past and was the one Jacobus had taken on his PCT trip, but I still was not reconciled to carrying a 7½-pound tent, so I continued to look for a lighter alternative.

When the *Backpacker* magazine "Gear Guide" came out in March, I eagerly checked their listings. In it were exactly 376 different tents, with detailed price and specification information for each, but the tents fell into the familiar pattern of weighing around five pounds for a two-person tent and seven to eight pounds, or more, for a three-person tent. Then, I noticed a listing for Stephenson's Warmlite. Could this be the same company that used to send me their catalogue 35 years ago? The company with naked women displaying avant-garde gear? I hurried to its website (www.warmlite.com), looking for some cheap thrills and maybe a lightweight tent, only to be greeted with a warning: "NOTICE. This site contains some nude pictures in natural settings. You have been warned!" Undeterred by the prospect of seeing attractive nude women in nature with Stephenson's gear, I clicked on. Yes, it was the same company, the same goofy ads with attractive naked women (and one man), the same dense explanations of their gear, AND some very lightweight tents. In fact, revolutionary lightweight tents. The Warmlite roomy (42 square feet) two-person 2X one-wall tent weighed only 2.33 pounds, and the two-person 2R two-wall tent only 2.75 pounds—roughly half the weight of most two-person tents, despite being 15 percent to 25 percent larger. The three-person 3X one-wall tent with 52 square feet of interior space weighed just 3.25 pounds, and the model 3R two-wall tent just 3.75 pounds—and Warmlite claimed they were stronger and more stable than other tents. Was Warmlite living in their own naked fantasy world, or had they broken all the rules that other tent manufacturers adhered to? Did the Warmlite tents work? I called Warmlite to see what I could learn.

After asking the woman who answered the phone whether she was wearing any clothes at that moment, I got more serious. I was immediately transferred to "Jack Stephenson, the founder of the company." Jack came on the line and the gruffness in his voice counseled me not to ask if he was naked, so I stuck to tents. I asked him, "What are you doing that is so different?" "How can you make such light tents?" "Are they sturdy?" "Can they withstand the abuse of a long trip?" "How do they do in high winds?" "Do they handle condensation well?" And a lot more questions of that type. As to each, Jack answered with great certitude and conviction: "I'm a former aerospace engineer who's been designing revolutionary backcountry equipment for more than 35 years. We make the best tents on the planet. They are the lightest tents you can find anywhere and the strongest. They have been used throughout the world, even in the Himalayas, and never have failed. We use revolutionary, thin 'ultra-high tenacity' rip-stop nylon coated with a durable silicone waterproof finish and the strongest poles used in any tent, despite their light weight. Our poles are 20 times stronger than the thin, flexible poles used in other tents and will stand up to wind and snow loads that would crush other tents." And, without my even asking, he explained the nudity: "My wife and I and my family are naturalists, which is why I have naked models—most of whom are my relatives—in the ads. If God wanted us to wear clothes, we would have been born with clothes."

"Jack," I replied, "I don't think that is your best argument. If God wanted us to use nylon tents, we wouldn't have to pay $500 for a Warmlite tent, he would have provided them to us for free." To which Jack responded, "Well, I guess you've got a point there."

I asked what the return policy was in case I didn't like the tent. "We don't have a return policy. The tents are custom-made for you and once you buy it, it is yours," he replied. I said, "Seeing it on a website is one thing, but how can I know what it is really like without setting one up and crawling inside?" "It's the best tent you'll ever buy. You won't want to return it," he said, once again with unyielding certitude. Despite enjoying my conversation with Jack, a genuine curmudgeon, I was leery of plunking down $500 for a tent that I hadn't seen and couldn't return, so I deferred the tent decision.

A month later, I was invited to join some people from the Southern Utah Wilderness Alliance on a canyoneering trip in the Escalante Canyon area. The trip would be led by Steve Allen, author of the best canyoneering and hiking books in Utah. In May, along with 10 other supporters and activists for Utah wilderness, I began a weeklong exploration of some of Steve's favorite canyons, including some not in his books. Steve turned out to be the most fabulous trip leader I've ever met, and the other people on the trip were very interesting as well.

One was Peter Metcalf, owner of Black Diamond, a

famous mountaineering gear and clothing company. During the first few days of the trip, I noticed how competent Peter was in the wilderness, how Steve asked him to take all the leads whenever we had to do a little technical climbing, and how well-equipped he was in his personal gear. One day we were walking together and I asked if he had ever heard of a little company named Warmlite.

"Know them? Last year, I tried to buy their company. They make great tents and equipment and I wanted to add them to our catalogue," replied Peter.

"Have you ever actually used one of their tents?" I asked.

"Absolutely. Last year I climbed Mt. McKinley and we used a Warmlite tent. It worked great, even in very high winds."

"Jack said the floors were made from very lightweight material and that worries me, what do you think?"

"I was concerned about the floors also and would prefer stronger material on the floors, but we were crawling in and out of the tents with crampons on and never punched any holes in the floors, so it is stronger than it appears," Peter advised.

What a coincidence. Small worldism strikes again!

When I returned from Utah, I called Warmlite, got Jack on the phone again, and told him I'd like to order a 3R tent with large side windows on both sides, which added five ounces. The Warmlite website stated that the seams were not seam-sealed but that a seam-sealing liquid was available, so I told Jack, "I'd like you to have the tent seam-sealed for me. I'll pay for this, of course." "We think you should seam-seal it yourself," Jack replied. "Why?" I asked. "If we seam-seal the tent for you, we're just going to charge an exorbitant price," Jack said. "Why would you charge an exorbitant price for this?' I inquired. "Because we think it is foolish to pay us for doing this," Jack replied. "In other words, you are trying to protect me from myself?" I asked. "I guess you could put it that way," Jack offered. "What's the exorbitant price?" I asked. "Fifty dollars for the whole tent," said Jack. "Well, I'm very busy and it's worth it to me to pay $50 and not have to do it myself, so please seam-seal it for me," I said. I didn't consider $50 exorbitant, but this certainly was the first time I've ever had someone selling something to me describe his price as "exorbitant," or try to discourage me from buying something I wanted. Like I said earlier, Jack Stephenson is a genuine iconoclast and curmudgeon.

Warmlite had an infinite variety of tent fabric colors, but I picked a light blue/dark blue tent that Jack had in stock in order to avoid a two- to three-month wait. It arrived in time for a weeklong whitewater canoe-camping trip on California's Trinity River I had planned with my wife, Jeanine, and another couple. The weather was great on this trip and we didn't try to set up the Warmlite tent until the sixth night. After a long day on the river we stopped at a really crappy campsite on private land that a local Hoopa Indian landowner was kind enough to let us camp on. After a long dinner and a couple of bottles of wine, we went to bed at midnight, only to find our sleeping bags covered with earwigs—an insect about ¾ of an inch long with two sharp pincers on its head. I wasn't familiar with earwigs and was inclined just to crawl into our bags, but our canoe-mates, Tamara and Keith, said (from the comfort and safety of their closed tent) that earwigs were dangerous—they can crawl inside ears and do serious damage. Earwigs in my ears didn't sound like a barrel of laughs, so I said to Jeanine, "This is the night to test our Warmlite tent." We pulled it out of its sack and began to read the dense and nearly incomprehensible instructions, trying repeatedly—but unsuccessfully—to get the aluminum tent poles that hold up the tent to slip into the tent fabric, as we fought off hundreds of earwigs who were trying to climb up our legs and arms. As we continued to flail away at the tent while Keith continued to pronounce the dangers of earwigs from inside his tent, I turned to Jeanine and said, "This is not exactly my idea of fun." After an hour of futility, and with the time now 1 a.m., we decided we had no choice but to do the ultimately humiliating act—walk three miles to the nearest town and look for a motel, which is what we did, arriving at 2:30 a.m. and making enough noise to wake up the proprietor. So, I'd have to say our first night with the Warmlite tent was not exactly a resounding success.

We brought the tent home, put it in the washing machine to get rid of all the earwigs, then set it up a month later in the backyard. Four live and apparently healthy earwigs crawled out. I guess they don't drown easily and can survive not eating for long periods of time. Persistent little buggers. In any case, I took them out into the street in front of our house, pointed them west, then went inside and sent an email to Keith and Tamara: "Attention—four earwigs sighted in Piedmont. Last seen on Glen Alpine Road heading directly toward your house."

After recovering from my second interaction with the little beasts, I attempted to set up the Warmlite tent. In daylight, without earwigs crawling all over me, the instructions made more sense, and, with Jacobus' and a friend's help, I succeeded in figuring out how to set up the tent. It actually is quite easy if you know how to do it. We then crawled in and out of the Warmlite 3R tent and evaluated it in relation to our North Face tent. The Warmlite certainly was big enough, much bigger in fact than our heavier North Face tent, but the Warmlite tent also was longer than our North Face tent and Jacobus wondered if we might have trouble fitting it into some tight tentsites. I recognized that could be a problem, but the Warmlite tent would save us over three pounds and we needed to go light, so we packed it. As it turned out, we encountered only one campsite where the length of the Warmlite was a problem, and this particular campsite had larger tentsites adjacent to it. The Warmlite 3R set up quickly and performed well on the trail, but the Warmlite tents are so roomy we could have carried the 2R two-person tent and saved an additional pound without sacrificing much comfort. On future long trips, I'll be carrying a Warmlite 2R.

Packs

The greatest innovator in frameless backpacks has been Gregory Packs. I bought one of Gregory's first frameless packs more than 20 years ago, and it served me well on many trips. But Gregory was purchased a number of years ago by a larger company and began to lose its lead in pack development, while other manufacturers emerged and sprinted ahead. For the JMT trip, I abandoned my trusty Gregory in favor of the Dana Design Terraplane, which Marmot Mountain Works, a dealer in Berkeley, carries, and which my sons, Leon and Jacobus, also used. The Dana Designs Terraplane has more volume (6,000 cubic inches), more features and more adjustments than the

Gregory, and is more stable on my back. My high opinion of this pack is shared by *Backpacker* magazine, which rated it numero uno in a weeklong backpacking pack comparison test in 1997, and its Gear Guide, which gave the Terraplane the first Editors Choice Gold Award, in 1999. The Terraplane has everything one could want in a pack, but at six pounds, nine ounces is not light.

For my Tahoe-to-Yosemite Trail hike a year later, I field-tested many large-volume packs and decided on the Kelty Haiku 5750. The Haiku has just one pocket on the top flap, has fewer adjustments, and is slightly less stable than the Dana Designs Terraplane. Also, it is made from lighter-weight nylon which probably won't stand up as well to heavy abuse as the heavy cordura material of the Terraplane, but at three pounds and 15 ounces, it is almost three pounds lighter. The hip and shoulder belts on the Haiku are comfortable and the volume at 5,750 cubic inches sufficient for long hikes. A couple more pockets for the Haiku would make gear more accessible, but such convenience is not worth three-plus pounds, in my opinion.

While 20 years ago, only one company was developing user-friendly frameless packs, the 2004 *Backpacker* magazine Gear Guide listed 50 companies currently manufacturing similar packs. I'm sure many are excellent. The problem with most of these packs is that the large-volume packs (i.e., 5,000 to 7,000 cubic inches) that are needed on long hikes typically weigh six to eight pounds, like the Dana Designs Terraplane.

There are a few exceptions, however. Lightweight large-volume packs include the following: Marmot Mountain Himalayan 80, www.marmot.com (5,100 cubic inches, three pounds, nine ounces); Mountainsmith Specter, www.mountainsmith.com (5,400 cubic inches, four pounds, four ounces); Trek Sport Outdoors Patagonia 80, www.treksportoutdoors.com (5,800 cubic inches, four pounds, seven ounces); Wookey Phoenix 90, www.wookey.com (5,800 cubic inches, four pounds, nine ounces).

In the past few years, encouraged by the emerging "go light" philosophy espoused by Ray Jardine and others, some people have begun to sew for themselves hyper-light packs. We saw one such pack on the JMT, carried by The Purple Hat and described in the hiking section of this book. There also is a company manufacturing such packs—GoLite (www.golite.com). GoLite's Gust, its 4,650-cubic-inch (size medium) backpack, weighs just one pound four ounces. The pack consists of a nylon sack, shaped somewhat like a pillow, with one zippered compartment at the back, and an extension on the top that is filled to the top to gain full capacity. There is some thin foam on the inside of the back of the pack, but no internal frame to support the load and transfer weight to the hips. Nearly all the weight must be carried on the shoulder straps, and the thin, light, waist-belt does little more than stabilize the pack and keep it from swaying. The pack is light and cheap ($100, compared to the $300–400 for a Dana Design or Gregory pack), but is designed to carry no more than 30 pounds, so you have to be fully committed to the "go light" philosophy. It also lacks features such as multiple outside pockets and padded waist-belts that the heavier packs have.

I tested the GoLite Gust backpack on a weekend trip. I packed it as though I was going on a weeklong trip and all my gear fit in, including a large bear canister. It was comfortable at first, but the more I walked the more having nearly all the weight on my shoulders began to wear on me. I also missed the adjustments that come with heavier, more complete packs, such as straps to pull the top of the pack closer to the shoulders in order to put weight closer to the body and a sternum strap that connects the two shoulder straps. The Gust also was hotter as the nylon of the pack sits directly on the back; heavier packs, such as my Kelty and Dana, have thick mesh cushions on the back which breathe well. The nylon against the back also tends to slide downward more than the cushioned mesh material on the Dana. And the Gust lacks features such as multiple pockets, which permit items to be packed outside the main section. But, to save five pounds of weight, some backpackers will want to consider it. My most serious concern is the 30-pound weight limit the manufacturer puts on the pack. This could be quite constraining for most backpackers and/or for long sections of trail. For me, it will be a struggle to get all my gear and food for a week down to a total of 30 pounds; what would I do if a section of trail took 10 days to complete and I had to carry more than 30 pounds? Would the pack handle the extra weight? Would my shoulders survive?

The GoLite Gust is not the ultimate pack but there is no question that ultralight packs are here to stay. In the years ahead, I expect to see a lot of innovation in lightweight backpacks, mainly because the backpacking public is going to demand it and because the current design of relatively heavy packs provides many opportunities to save weight. Maybe the ultimate pack for me will be some yet-to-be-designed compromise of lightweight pack fabric and creature comforts such as a padded hipbelt, a light internal frame made of graphite or some other light, yet strong, material, and more pockets. Such a pack might weigh three pounds—heavier than the GoLite Gust, but still less than half the weight of most large-volume packs.

Footwear

There is almost an infinite number of boots for hiking. The types of boots to consider for hiking the JMT range from heavy mountaineering boots to lightweight running shoes, and I saw both extremes on the feet of the JMT hikers we met. Surprisingly, the tilt was heavily toward very lightweight boots, even the low-cut variety, over traditional mountaineering boots or rugged backpacking boots. I think there are several reasons for this. First, the lightweight boots with fabric tops weigh 2 to 2½ pounds less than high-top, rugged, leather backpacking boots, and 3 to 3½ pounds less than mountaineering boots. It's an axiom that "one pound on your feet is worth five pounds on your back," and many have gotten that message. Second, the softer fabric tops are easier on the feet— much less prone to rub the tender tootsies and cause blisters. Lightweight boots dry quickly when wet, and may even be comfortable enough to wear as camp shoes, although that raises additional issues.

The disadvantages of lightweight and/or low-cut hiking boots are obvious. For one, the flexible sole that contributes to its comfort also is a weaker barrier to the thousands of sharp rocks that you encounter on the trail every day. Should you land on a rock the wrong way or too hard, you could bruise a foot, impairing your hiking for days or longer. Second, the flexible uppers, as well as the low-cut designs, provide less protection against ankle sprains. I have played basketball all my life in low-cut shoes and have had almost no problems with ankle sprains so I consider my ankles to be pretty strong, yet I sprained or twisted both ankles (without even knowing how I did it) on the 20th day of my JMT hike. Were it not for the miracle of arnica, a homeopathic remedy for sprains and strains, my hiking would have been delayed at least a day. Hiking in lightweight boots will, at a minimum, require that you step more carefully and alertly than would be necessary if hiking in mountaineering boots. And lightweight fabric boots provide little protection against rain, so if much rain is anticipated, only leather boots impregnated with Nik-Wax, silicon, or some other type of waterproofing, or fabric boots with a Gore-Tex lining, will keep feet dry. This raises a collateral issue. The more sealed and watertight your boots are, the hotter they are going to be on your feet. Heat is the enemy of feet, as it causes sweating, wet socks, and blisters.

To resolve the conflict betwen choosing foot protection and comfort, I selected medium weight, moderately flexible, high-top, full-leather boots made by Merrell. The leather permitted me to waterproof the boots, while the flexibility of the sole and the leather uppers made the boots comfortable enough, along with other protective measures I took, I didn't get blisters for four weeks. However, on my Tahoe-to-Yosemite Trail hike the following year, I switched to low-cut lightweight fabric boots with a good lug sole and the lighter boots performed very well. While on the JMT, I queried everyone I met who was hiking with very light footwear, including one young man who had hiked the 700-mile Colorado Trail with his lightweight boots before hitting the JMT, and all said their lightweight shoes were working well for them. Unless I am

Top: Jacobus next to John Muir Trail sign
Bottom: Our Stephenson's Warmlite tent alongside the Lyell

Top Left: Leaving Tuolumne Meadows Campground
Top Right: The largest pack we saw on the John Muir Trail
Bottom: Bear box at Rae Lakes

hiking in very wet country or where much rain is anticipated, my future hiking will be in lightweight boots.

A pair of boots that came as close to perfection as any
boots I've ever seen or used were a pair of Merrell low-
cut, full-leather boots with a mountaineering sole (somewhat stiff, with a steel shank). I took these boots to Nepal
as a backup to my Merrell mountaineering boots, which I
expected to wear every day on the steep, rocky trails. But,
instead of my broken-in mountaineering boots, I found
myself walking day after day in my new low-cut boots;
the uppers were so comfortable and flexible, and the soles
so substantial, that I never got blisters and never bruised
my feet. The only time I wore my mountaineering boots
was above 16,500 feet, where the snow often was too
deep for low-cuts, even with gaiters. For reasons that I
cannot even fathom, Merrell discontinued making this
incredible boot six years ago—replacing it with low-cut
leather boots with flexible uppers but also soft soles—and
I haven't been able to find a perfect replacement. Merrell,
are you listening? Please bring back those great boots.

Choosing a pair of boots does not end the issue. You
still need to consider camp shoes and/or footwear for
lakes and streams. On past trips, for camp shoes I have
carried a lightweight pair of running shoes. They are comfortable, allowing you to get out of boots that are usually
damp with sweat by the end of a hiking day and let your
feet dry out. Also, they make getting in and out of lakes
and streams with rocky bottoms easier and avoid the risk
that feet might get cut or bruised slipping on underwater
rocks. And, in spring and early summer, when streams are
high and sometimes dangerous, these shoes permit hiking
boots to stay dry in the pack, yet provide enough support

and cushion to walk in fast water over rocky bottoms. The downside is that when they get wet, they become much heavier to carry and they don't dry very quickly—often 24 hours or more—making them often unusable as daily camp shoes.

For the JMT, I considered carrying three pairs of shoes: medium-weight boots for daily hiking, lightweight running shoes for camp shoes and as a backup for hiking in case I developed serious blisters, and super-light synthetic river kayaking booties, water crossings, and swimming. Jacobus convinced me he had a better idea. Instead of running shoes and kayaking booties, he recommended taking just a pair of Tevas. Tevas are lightweight, dry quickly, the soles provide good cushion against river rocks, and, when used as camp shoes, permit feet to dry out and toughen. The only downside is that any socks you wear with the Tevas in camp tend to get dirty, but no system is perfect and that downside was relatively insubstantial (to solve this problem, I used a dirty pair of inner socks as my camp socks). In any case, I took Jacobus' recommendation. It worked well in every respect: the Tevas functioned perfectly for walking in water, dried quickly on the back of my pack so they always were dry by the time we got into camp, and wearing them in camp allowed my feet to dry out, greatly contributing to my "no-blisters-for-four weeks" success.

Socks, Gaiters, and Insoles

The first thing John Wooden, the great UCLA basketball coach, did each year was instruct his players about how to put on their socks. He felt socks were that important to the success of his basketball teams. Socks are at least as important for hiking.

For backpacking, I've always worn a lightweight pair of Ultimax inner-socks, along with a heavier pair of hiking socks, with my boots. In the past, I have worn thick socks made by Wigwam from synthetic materials as my heavy socks; they provide good cushion for my feet and always seemed comfortable to put on, which the book *Fitness for Feet* confirmed. But, Jacobus recommended not wearing socks made from synthetic materials because synthetic socks tend to be hot on the feet. Instead, Jacobus and the book recommended all-wool socks as the outer hiking socks. I took this advice, buying Smart Wool mid-weight hiking socks. They stayed cooler and my feet stayed drier. As a consequence, I now join Jacobus in recommending all-wool outer socks. The only downside, compared to the synthetics, is that the wool socks tend to wear faster. I think the all-wool socks we took on the JMT might have lasted the full month of hiking, but we took no chances and included extra socks in our resupply provisions.

I have used gaiters cross-country skiing in the winter and whenever I expected to encounter snow in other seasons, but I never had used gaiters while hiking in the summer until I read *Fixing Your Feet,* which argued that gaiters should be worn hiking in all seasons to keep out dirt and sand, which gets into socks and grinds away at skin creating blisters. The book's point made perfect sense, so I bought a pair of lightweight, low-cut gaiters made by Outdoor Research (they call them Flex-Tex Low Gaiters). Unlike winter gaiters, which reach to the knee and are made from waterproof fabric, these low gaiters were made from breathable spandex and nylon, which made them fit tightly over boots, yet remain relatively cool. I noticed immediately that my socks stayed cleaner, and I didn't end each hiking day with sand or dirt between my toes. This helped to protect my feet from blisters, as I didn't get any for four weeks.

Lastly, on the subject of feet, backpackers should consider buying a pair of good-quality insoles for their boots. All boots come equipped with insoles, of course, but the insoles tend to be pretty flimsy and inconsequential. Superfeet (www.superfeet.com) and Birkenstock are two companies making better quality insoles, which are available in all sizes and can be trimmed to fit any size boot. These insoles provide good support, particularly the instep and heel, which improves comfort and stability. This can help protect against twisting when feet land on rocks at odd angles and prevent possible ankle and/or foot sprains. The Superfeet insoles come in several thicknesses, so you can experiment and decide which thickness works best in your boots.

Sleeping Bags and Pads

John Muir carried neither a sleeping bag nor a sleeping pad. For warmth in the backcountry, he would build a fire, spread leaves and branches on the ground, and roll up in his wool coat, tending the fire throughout the night to stay warm. But we are not John Muir.

There are two choices for the type of sleeping bag you will need to take—a synthetic-fill bag or a down-fill bag. The synthetic bags are significantly cheaper and retain their loft when wet better than down, but in all other respects the down-fill bags are superior. The down bags provide more warmth for less weight, compress smaller making packing easier, and last much longer. In moderate use, a good down-fill bag can last 15 years or more; amortized over such long usage, the cost is moderate even for the best down bags.

Down is rated by "fill power." One ounce of the best available down will fill up to 900 cubic inches (called "900-fill"); not surprisingly, the fluffiest 900-fill is more expensive than 600-fill. I'd say any bag with a 600-fill or more rating is going to be a decent bag; go for the 750+ fill rated bag if your pocketbook can afford it, as it will provide more warmth for less weight.

Most down sleeping bags have an outer covering of nylon, which works fine. Some of the premium bags made by such manufacturers as Marmot and Moonstone use Gore Dryloft as the outer shell for some of their bags. Dryloft provides protection from water, while being breathable, and it offers slightly more warmth for the same amount of fill than nylon. If you are going to be sleeping outside, where rain, dew, and/or dampness may land on your bag, a Dryloft outer shell provides added protection against water. In some circumstances, this could be a significant advantage, as the last thing you can ever let happen to a down-fill bag is to let the down-fill get wet. Wet down is useless. It bunches up into little balls and provides little or no insulation. To make matters worse, wet down is very difficult to dry out. Normally, drying requires a heavy-duty clothes dryer, and since there are few laundromats in the backcountry, one way or another you need to keep your down-fill dry.

That raises the issue of how much down-fill you need. Bags are given temperature ratings by each manufacturer, but there are no industry standards for determining such ratings. I'd say the ratings manufacturers give their bags are accurate relative to their own selection of bags, but not in comparison to other manufacturers' bags and claims about their bags. Also, to state the obvious, some people sleep warm and some always seem cold—and manufactur-er temperature ratings do not factor in personal differ-ences. Thus, like beauty, temperature may be in the eye of the beholder, and the bottom line is that you have to try out bags in the high country yourself to determine how much loft and down-fill you need to keep you warm in the conditions you expect to be hiking in. Some backpacking equipment stores rent sleeping bags, and renting is one way to test bags. Even that is not perfect, as a bag that has been heavily rented may have much less loft than the same bag when new, and thus be colder to sleep in. The range of bags you should consider are those rated 25 degrees down to 0 degrees. That doesn't mean you are likely to encounter 0 degree conditions—it is possible, but highly unlikely—but some people will need a bag rated 0 degrees even on a 20-degree night, particularly when sleeping outside.

I own three sleeping bags, which I have acquired over the years, each made by Marmot Mountain, Ltd.: the Arroyo, rated 35 degrees, weight 1 pound, 12 ounces; the Pinnacle Dryloft, rated 15 degrees, 2 pounds, 7 ounces; and the Couloir Dryloft, rated 0 degrees, 3 pounds, 1 ounce. I use the 35-degree bag for spring and fall desert hiking and river trips in Utah and Arizona. In such warm climates, even with a very light bag, I often have part of my body hanging outside the bag when I sleep. The 0-degree bag covers my rare winter cross-country ski camp-ing trips, as well as expected low temps late in the back-packing season. My 15-degree bag is my general-purpose backpacking bag.

On our JMT trip, Jacobus and I hiked the first two weeks with our 15-degree bags, then switched to our 0-degree bags at Muir Trail Ranch, in anticipation of higher elevations and colder temperatures for the last half of our trip, which ended in early October. In retrospect, I think switching to the heavier bags was unnecessary. For the coldest nights, we could have slept with more clothing on and been fine, and each saved 10 ounces of weight.

For a sleeping pad, I long have carried Therm-A-Rest self-inflating pads, and Jacobus and I both took Therm-A-Rest Ultralite ¾ length (20" by 47" and 1 inch thick) pads, weighing one pound each. Therm-A-Rest makes larger, thicker, and more comfortable self-inflating pads, but I never would consider any but the Ultralight for a backpacking trip because of the added weight of the thicker pads. The Therm-A-Rest pads easily inflate and deflate, provide good insulation from cold ground, and are reasonably comfortable. They also are compact when deflated and easy to pack inside your pack, which is where I suggest you pack it so it doesn't get punctured by a branch or rock. They are not perfect, however, as I have had a couple of them puncture and deflate in my 20 or so years of hiking with them. Once deflated, they are useless, unless you have brought a patch kit, which I now always carry. Putting a patch on one is no more difficult than patching a bike tire, but the kit weighs an extra ounce or two. If you are willing to carry a patch kit, and patch any punctures, the Therma-A-Rest is a good choice for a pad—indeed, it is by far the most popular pad carried on backcountry trails these days.

On our JMT hike, I saw a number of backpackers carrying the Therm-A-Rest Z-Lite foam mattress. This is not a self-inflating air mattress, like the Ultralight, but simply a type of corrugated foam. The hikers I talked to were satisfied with the comfort of the Z-Lite, although it was not as cushy as the self-inflating Ultralight. The advantages of the Z-Lite are that it is cheaper, it doesn't puncture, and it is a few ounces lighter. It is a little bulky, however, so you probably would have to strap it on the outside of your pack.

Trekking Poles

No one should hike the JMT, or any long trail, without trekking poles. That is a pretty categorical statement and one I never would have made a few years ago. Then in 1998, I planned a hiking trip to Nepal with my son Leon, and in talking to people who had been there, everyone said, "Take trekking poles." I thought they were for wimps and sissies, but one of my mountaineering friends told me, "Reinhold Messner uses trekking poles on all of his approaches to big climbs, and he's no wimp." No, he isn't, he's just the greatest mountaineer who has ever walked the planet, so I thought, "If Reinhold Messner uses trekking poles, maybe I should try them," and I did. They were wonderful on the steep trails of Nepal. They gave my upper body exercise, provided some forward thrust when climbing (my estimate is 10 percent to 15 percent of what my legs did), cushioned my knees when hiking steeply downhill, and provided stability crossing streams and balancing on rocks. They also can double as tent or tarp poles. I now hike with them everywhere, even on short day hikes, and would feel naked without them. No, I don't sleep with them.

The evidence in favor of trekking poles is not just anecdotal; it now has some scientific basis. In separate studies, scientists at the Universities of Massachusetts and Wisconsin and at Steadman-Hawkins Sports Medicine Foundation in Colorado have found that using trekking poles reduces the risk of injury and tendinitis in knees, calves, thighs, and hips, as well as reducing fatigue.

There now are many trekking poles on the market in the United States. The ones Jacobus and I took on the JMT were the Leki Super Makalu Anti-Shock poles, made of aluminum, and weighing 11 ounces per pole. Leki makes a slightly lighter pole, the Ultralite TI, from aluminum and titanium, but it lacks the anti-shock feature which cushions pole placement and is particularly nice on steep downhill sections, especially for those of us who have had knee operations. The Makalu, like most trekking poles, collapses in three sections, which makes the poles packable. My only caution in using these poles is not to tighten them too much, as temperature changes sometimes can make them hard to loosen and adjust. You may want to shorten the poles when going uphill and lengthen them when hiking downhill or crossing streams.

Bear Canisters

When I began backpacking eons ago, no one thought much about bears. They were picturesque, but they didn't bother people and didn't steal food. Decades of humans traveling in the wilderness and not protecting their food—and in many cases even burying unused food—has taught bears to associate food with humans, with backpackers, with you! As a consequence, when you walk into the backcountry now, just assume you've got a big "FOOD" painted on your forehead. Not only do bears associate you with food, they have figured out where you keep it and how to get it. It used to be that you could hang food over a branch or bear cable 12 to 15 feet off the ground, tie your rope onto a nearby tree, or balance two bags over a branch or cable, and the bears would never get to it. These techniques, particularly the balance method, still work sometimes, but more often our modern California bears will associate the rope with the food bag and pull it down, or, failing that, climb the tree or cable and snatch the food. This used to really piss me off. Twenty years ago, I even chased a bear and her cubs who had bagged my food into the bushes, yelling and screaming at them to return my food, thinking that if I caught them I'd rip the food sack out of their thieving paws. Today, this type of behavior is likely to get you chewed up, or at least badly scratched. In fact, a few weeks before we began hiking the JMT, there were newspaper reports of two separate incidents of backpackers near the JMT getting mauled by bears because they had tried to retrieve food sacks taken by bears. Read on:

Two Hikers Clawed By Bears While Trying to Scare Them

SEQUOIA NATIONAL PARK (AP)—Two backpackers trying to protect their food were clawed by black bears at national parks, one at Sequoia and the other at Kings Canyon, authorities said Friday. The hikers were not seriously hurt in the incidents last week at remote backcountry lakes in the high Sierra.

In both instances, the men had improperly stored food in trees and then tried to scare the bears away once they had reached the food, park spokeswoman Kris Fister said Friday. "If you're in a situation when they've already got your food, it will be very difficult to get the bears away from it," Fister said.

One backpacker was injured Aug. 9 at Soldier Lakes in Sequoia National Park when the startled bear bolted from the tree and ran over him.

The second incident happened Aug. 10 at Kearsarge Lakes in adjacent Kings Canyon National Park when two backpackers tried to roust a bear by yelling and throwing rocks. One man was clawed as the bear ran away. The same man was clawed again while trying to frighten the animal. He was treated at a hospital and released.

No woman would be dumb enough to act like this, so, men, keep your testosterone under control, at least in the wilderness, and don't chase bears! Accept your losses, hike out for replacement food, and next time carry a bear canister.

Bear canisters now are required in the backcountry of national parks. Bear canisters save you the trouble of trying to hang food in bear-proof locations, which you probably won't be able to find anyway, as well as the indignity and delay of having to hike out for more food. Most important, they protect bears and other wild animals from becoming dependent on human food and allow them to remain wild, as they should be. The downside to bear canisters is that they are bulky and each weighs two pounds, or more. You must carry them, so get used to it.

The most common bear canister in use today is the Garcia canister, known formally as the Model 812 Backpackers' Cache, a heavy-plastic cylinder that bears cannot get their mouths around and cannot break or crush. I have seen videos of bears not only trying to crush the Garcia in their mouths and with their paws, but also throwing the Garcia over the edge of cliffs onto rocks to see if the canister will break. These bears are resourceful and formidable, but the Garcia stands up to the punishment. The downside to the Garcia is that it weighs 2 pounds, 11 ounces, and carries only about three to four days worth of food for two people; thus, if you have a week or more between resupplies, you need to carry at least two canisters, and maybe three. The Garcia canister costs about $75, and many national parks rent them for a nominal fee; some even let backpackers borrow them for free.

I was not happy with the prospect of carrying an extra five pounds, or more, so I searched for a lighter alternative and found the Ursack, which was advertised as a "bear resistant" food storage sack made from "bullet-proof fabric," weighing just five ounces for the small size (a claimed 650 cubic inches) and seven ounces for the large size (1100 cubic inches). The Ursack website (www.ursack.com) even had a video of a bear trying to chew the Ursack and not succeeding in breaking it open. Voila! An easy way to save weight!. Unfortunately, the claims proved to be too good to be true, as three weeks before our JMT trip was to begin, Sierra bears busted open several Ursacks carried by backpackers, and Yosemite National Park revoked the Ursack's conditional approval as a bear canister.

The demise of the Ursack prompted a quick search for an alternative to the Garcia. On the Yosemite National Park website, www.wild-ideas.net, I located the Bearikade. The Bearikade costs about twice as much as the Garcia but weighs nearly a pound less and comes in two sizes. It is not a battleship like the Garcia, but it is well-built and was rated Conditionally Approved by the national parks. Conditional approval is obtained by passing a visual inspection, an impact test, and a zoo test; full approval also requires three months of field-testing—i.e., by wild bears. To save 2+ pounds, I bought two large Bearikade canisters, which we carried until we hit Kings Canyon National Park. There, we were able to find bear boxes to store food overnight. Our Bearikade never was tested on our trip, perhaps because bears are beginning to understand they can't break into them, so they don't even try (if this theory is accurate, maybe we could all carry bear canisters made out of light cardboard, painted to look like the Garcia). Of course, the Bearikade hasn't yet been tested by The Great Mutant Bear, which roams the Sierras and provides opportunity for scary (and untrue) campfire tales.

Water and Water Filters

Water is so abundant along the JMT, even in dry years, that only once did we walk for more than three hours without finding water available. To carry our supply, we used water bladders with hoses that extended out of the top of our packs, over our shoulders, and attached to our shoulder straps. This eliminates the need to stop and pull a water bottle out of your pack, or having your hiking partner stop to get it out for you, and allows you to have water any time you want. I carried a Platypus Hoser 2-liter water bladder, which would last most of a hiking day; on days when I anticipated there might be a long stretch between water sources, I also carried a 1-liter Nalgene water bottle, which doubled at meals as something I could drink from or mix powdered beverages in. The Platypus bladders are very lightweight, don't emit a plastic taste, and are quite durable. Mine worked perfectly for a month.

We also carried a PUR Hiker water filter for filtering water. I have used many different water filters in the back-country (including Katadyn, Sweetwater, and MSR filters) and have found the PUR the easiest to use and one of the lightest filters on the market (11 ounces). Many back-packers, however, think that even 11 ounces is too much to carry, and instead bring lightweight iodine tablets, such as Potable Agua, to purify water. Personally, I consider the idea of poisoning Sierra water with foul-tasting iodine to be abhorrent, but you may prefer to save 10 ounces and not mind that your iodine-laced water on the JMT will taste awful.

The third alternative is just to drink out of the streams and lakes. I thought this choice had vanished under the onslaught of pack animals and backpackers, but three weeks into our JMT trip we met a wilderness ranger who told us that the fear of giardia and other water-borne afflictions was bunk, at least in the Sierras when far away from cows and horses, and that she, her husband, and their co-workers had been drinking water right out of Sierra streams for 20 years without a single case of giar-dia, or anything else. Maybe they all had cast-iron stom-achs. I can't recommend that you not filter water—indeed, I always carry a filter—but I have no fear of drinking directly out of streams high in the Sierras where I am con-fident pack animals have not grazed and backpackers haven't camped right next to streams above me. Once again, you must decide on the appropriate level of risk for you. Or maybe, as Clint Eastwood said so memorably in another context, "You've got to ask yourself one ques-tion: 'Do I feel lucky?'"

Cooking Gear

One lightnik we met carried no cooking equipment because he didn't cook anything—he carried dried cereals, fruits, and nuts. That certainly is the lightest and fastest approach to cooking I can think of. However, I once had an experience on a 10-day backpacking trip in the San Juan Mountains of Colorado that prevents me from following this path. My wife, Jeanine, and I and another couple from Berkeley decided that since we all loved gorp (mostly dried fruit and nuts) so much, we'd bring a big bag and have it for lunch each day. For 10 days, all we ate for lunch were handfuls of gorp. When I finished that trip, I was so sick of the stuff I vowed never to eat it again, and I now can report, nearly 30 years later, I have kept my vow. No gorp has passed my lips in 30 years. I can't even imagine the greater torture of eating dried food three times a day.

In anticipation of hiking the JMT, Jacobus had bought me an Evernew titanium cook set for Christmas. These two pots (2.7 and 2.0 quarts) with lids were very light (about half the weight of stainless steel). They also had a Teflon coating. The Teflon was marvelous. It made washing dishes (which was mostly my job) about 10 times easier than scrubbing burnt food off the bottom of a steel or aluminum pot. This was particularly nice when I was washing pots at night at least 300 feet away from water, which is what Jacobus— my resident environmentalist—insisted on.

Wood fires are not permitted above 10,000 feet in most locations on the JMT, so you will have to bring a stove. For nearly 40 years, I have been faithful to my little Svea 123 stove (1 pound, 3 ounces), but for this trip, we took Jacobus' MSR Dragonfly stove (1 pound, 1 ounce), and I must say, it outperformed the Svea. The Dragonfly is lighter and burns more consistently at low temperatures. Because it is connected to the gas bottle, you don't lose gas trying to pour gas into a small opening in the stove tank and it doesn't run out of fuel in the middle of cooking. Even lighter is the MSR Whisperlite (14 ounces). The downside to the Whisperlite is that it doesn't simmer very well. To light our stove, we brought a BIC lighter. Both the Dragonfly and the Whisperlite use white gas, often sold as camp fuel.

Super-light stove options include the Snow Peak Gigapower and the MSR Pocketrocket. Each weighs around three ounces and uses disposable gas canisters filled with butane or propane. Each canister weighs about eight ounces and you would need three canisters to equal the burn time of one 22-ounce can of white gas, so the net weight savings of the butane/propane system is nearly a pound. Three canisters are bulkier than one 22-ounce can of white gas, but you can crush the canisters after use. Propane and butane stoves don't work well in very cold weather—so don't take them snow camping—but this should not be a problem on the JMT in summer or fall. These two stoves are not as stable for holding pots as the MSR Dragonfly and Whisperlite, but propane/butane stoves simmer well and are easy to ignite and use.

On the JMT, we also carried a MSR gas bottle made from titanium. The aluminum gas bottles perform just as well, but the titanium bottle weighs two ounces less for the same volume and it doesn't dent as easily as aluminum. We found that one 650 ml bottle was sufficient for up to a week of cooking our breakfasts and dinners. Of course, we ate dehydrated dinners, which cook quickly; if you were to try to take and cook non-dehydrated foods, you would need to carry more gas.

We each brought a Nalgene bowl with a lid for our morning oatmeal and dinners; the lid allowed us to pour hot water on oatmeal in the bowl and let it cook, without even dirtying a pot. Inside the bowl, I carried a Nalgene cup, with the useless handle sawed off to save an ounce. For utensils, we each carried one lexan spoon. We both had pocket knifes to cut the salami we carried for lunches.

Clothing

This is a huge topic. Instead of trying to cover the entire range of choices, I'd like to explain the choices we made and why we made them.

As rain gear, I carried Marmot Osprey pants and parka, which are high-quality Gore-Tex products. In retrospect, and in light of the good weather we had, I could have carried lighter rain gear and been fine. Marmot makes extremely lightweight, inexpensive rain gear they call Pre-Cip. The Pre-Cip line is less well-made, might not hold up well over time, and is not as breathable as Gore-Tex, but we each could have saved 1½ pounds carrying Pre-Cip rain pants and parka, which is what I will do on future trips in the Sierras. Hiking in the Cascades or Rockies, where rain is frequent, might compel better rain gear, but I think you will be safe on the JMT with lightweight gear.

Another option is a poncho, or even an umbrella, which we saw some Brits carrying. A poncho will be lighter, but rain pants and a parka serve a double role by providing protection from wind, adding a layer of warmth. Although we never had to contend with rain, we wore our rain pants and parkas each evening for warmth. A poncho doesn't serve this function very well and an umbrella doesn't serve it at all.

I hiked in a pair of black nylon Teva shorts, which have swimsuit netting inside and saved the need, and weight, of underpants. This not only saved weight, it provided good ventilation during hot hiking days and permitted me to swim without worrying about cotton underpants getting wet. Nylon shorts dry out quickly. Since the shorts were black, they stayed clean—meaning, they appeared to stay clean. Sometimes I also hiked in either a T-shirt or a lightweight Ex Officio long-sleeve shirt made of 55% cotton and 45% nylon. I should have left the T-shirt at home and saved seven ounces. The T-shirt didn't really perform any role the long-sleeve shirt couldn't have done just as well. Because the days are warm, and hiking with a pack creates a lot of body heat, I rarely wore anything on my upper body. When weather turned cool, the cotton/nylon long-sleeve shirt worked fine, as rolling up the sleeves and opening or closing the front buttons permitted a good range of temperature adjustments.

As soon as the sun began to set, I would put on a pair of medium-weight Patagonia Capilene thermal bottoms under my Teva shorts (which I wore at night for the pockets), and my rain pants. I also wore a Patagonia Capilene thermal top, my long-sleeve shirt, a Marmot wind shirt, a medium-weight down parka, my rain parka, if necessary for additional warmth, and a heavy fleece hat. This collection was sufficient to keep me warm in all conditions, including the coldest breezy nights at high elevations with no campfire in September or October. If I had been hiking in July or August, I would have substituted a fleece jacket for the down parka and saved 10 ounces. I took a pair of Patagonia fingerless fleece gloves. Summer and fall are not really cold enough to require full gloves, and fingerless gloves permit hands to be fully functional.

Sun Protection

Unless you are actively pursuing a case of melanoma, you are going to need a good sun hat. More than half the JMT is above 10,000 feet, where the ozone layer is thinner, the sun more intense, and there are few, if any, trees to provide shade. As Dick Vitale might say, "It's you and the sun, baby."

For protection from too much sun, I took an REI Solarweave Sierra Hat, which basically is a baseball-style hat made from light nylon with about 10 inches of material hanging from the sides and back to protect ears and neck. REI claims it provides SPF 30+ sun protection, the lightweight nylon makes it cool, and wearing it will have you looking like a JMT version of Lawrence of Arabia. Jacobus wore a wide-brim nylon hat made by Outdoor Research called the Sonora Sombrero. We were Lawrence and José going down the trail, but neither of us got burned on our face, ears, or neck.

You will also need to take a good SPF 30+ sunscreen. We used Avon's Skin So Soft, which offers the side benefit of warding off bugs, plus it isn't greasy and it doesn't have the toxic smell that many bug juices have. I also carried sunscreen lip balm, rated SPF 30, which I applied periodically throughout the day.

Lastly, you will want to have a pair of sunglasses. We experienced so much sun and good weather, that I wore my sunglasses nearly all the time during the day. My

Oakley sunglasses had polarized lenses, which provide great clarity when looking at water and in high mountain environments.

Flashlight

Jacobus and I agreed that headlamps were far more convenient to use than hand-held flashlights, but then we parted ways. Jacobus carried a battleship of a flashlight, the Petzel Zoom, which is a headlamp with a large light and large special battery worn at the back of the head, weighing nearly a pound. I carried the Petzel Tikka, which weighed in at just 2½ ounces. The Tikka uses LED lights on the front, which conserve batteries and disperse light well; Jacobus' Zoom had a bigger light, which provided better distance penetration, but it dispersed light less well than the Tikka for reading and close work. Despite using just three AAA batteries, compared to the Zoom's mega-battery, the Tikka's light actually outlived the larger Zoom. In fact, Petzel claims the Tikka's light will last 180 hours, but I found after about 10 hours of use, the light power progressively dimmed. In any case, the Tikka provided sufficient light for two weeks, despite the shorter days and longer nights of fall. After two weeks of lugging around his much heavier headlamp, Jacobus exchanged it for a Tikka that arrived in a resupply box. There is now an improved version, the Petzel Tikka Plus, with three brightness settings and an on-off button that never depresses accidentally; the Black Diamond Zenix with three settings, including Hyperbright, claimed to be five times brighter than normal LED bulbs (4.4 ounces); and the Princeton TEC Scout, using four lithium coin cells and weighing just 1.9 ounces.

As a backup flashlight, I took a Photon Micro Light. It weighs ¼ ounce. Photon claims the batteries last 120 hours, but I'm skeptical of that claim; even if they do last that long, I suspect the useful life is more like 10–20 hours. In any case, we met one hiker, The Purple Hat man, who was hiking the JMT carrying just the Photon Micro Light. He was doing a lot of night hiking, so the Photon might be a credible alternate to the Tikka. At only ¼ ounce, I suppose you could carry several. If you do buy the Photon, get the model with the on-off switch so you don't have to squeeze it constantly to get light.

First-Aid Kit

Adventure Medical Kits and REI make first-aid kits that contain the essentials for backpacking. We carried the REI Hiker, which weighs about six ounces. To the standard kit, we added some homeopathic remedies and a CPR mask. Jacobus is well-trained in first-aid and holds a Wilderness First Responder certificate (the industry-standard for wilderness trip leaders). I know little more than what I learned many years ago when I got my Boy Scout first-aid merit badge. For those with my level of first-aid knowledge, or less, the ready-made first-aid kits come with booklets that explain how to handle most first-aid situations. Of course, it would be better to take a first-aid course; one-day courses are offered by the Red Cross, Wilderness Medical Associates, and the Wilderness Medical Institute.

Maps

Although the JMT, and adjacent feeder trails, are well-marked, you will need to take topographical maps. You could collect all the 15-minute U.S.G.S. topographical maps that cover the JMT, but that would be a lot of maps and a lot of extra paper and weight to carry. The better alternative is to buy the "John Muir Trail Map-Pack," by Tom Harrison Maps, 2 Falmouth Cove, San Rafael CA 94901-4465, 800/265-9090, 415/456-7940, www.tomharrison-maps.com. This 13-page, waterproof, shaded-relief set of topographical maps weighs just two ounces and highlights the complete JMT. We never carried all the maps at one time; instead, we had maps for each section of our hike in our resupply boxes, thereby saving more than an ounce. You laugh, but an ounce is an ounce.

In addition to maps, we carried a compass and a copy of the north to south trail descriptions from the book *Guide to the John Muir Trail,* by Thomas Winnett and Kathy Morey, Wilderness Press, which we found accurate and useful. Note, we carried only 35 pages of the book, since much of the book is filled with maps that are inferior to the Tom Harrison maps and other information not needed on the trail.

Toiletries

I carried very little in the way of toiletries: a toothbrush, small tube of toothpaste, small towel made from super-absorbent material, and liquid biodegradable soap for use on bodies, pots, and utensils. I carried a small trowel, one roll of toilet paper for each section, and two Ziploc bags—one for the toilet paper roll, and the other for used toilet paper, which must be packed out. Jacobus lightened his pack by not carrying any toilet paper, preferring to use smooth sticks and rocks. I guess I'm just too domesticated for that system, but I know others, including Outward Bound, recommend it.

Camera and Film

Many years ago, I never traveled in the backcountry without a Nikon camera and two or three lenses, which, cumulatively, weighed three to four pounds, depending on the lenses taken, or even more if I took a tripod (which no serious photographer ever would be without). As time went on, I decided that I didn't like carrying that much extra weight and spending a lot of time on photography was a distraction and a delay. This was compounded by the fact that I almost never watched the thousands of slides I was accumulating. As a consequence, for the last five years, I've either carried no camera, or a simple Canon Elph, which weighs just five ounces, costs about $80, and takes reasonably decent photos. It is small enough to put in a shirt or pant pocket and simple enough to use without much setup time. The photos in this book were taken with the Elph, so decide for yourself if they are any good. On the JMT, I carried one 40-shot roll per section of trail. This amount of film was sufficient to remind me of the trip.

Miscellaneous Items

Eyeshades (one ounce) were useful for those times when Jacobus might be reading at night and I wanted to sleep past sunrise. I brought extra Ziploc bags for our garbage and for trash picked up along the trail, and to store things such as liquid soap and sunscreen. I carried a handkerchief and a small Swiss Army knife (Executive model, one ounce) in my pocket. Both have many uses. The handkerchief is good for wiping the brow on a hot day, for dipping in a stream and washing your face, for tying around the neck to protect against sunburn, to use as a napkin at

meals, etc. The Swiss Army knife was used for slicing salami, cutting rope and string, the scissors for cutting thread
and my beard, the toothpick for picking teeth, the tweez-
ers for splinters, etc. I took cheap reading glasses for reading the map, trail description and book, an REI
"Weatherproof Journal" and golf pencil for recording the
hike, and cash, a credit card, driver's license, and medical
insurance card. Also a little duct tape, because no one
should ever be without duct tape.

Extras I Found Useful

There are those who reject the idea of carrying any type of
timepiece into wilderness; "Get in tune with the rhythms of
nature and not be guided by clocks," they argue. I respect
that opinion, but it doesn't work for me. I want to know
what time it is, where I am, how fast or slow I'm hiking,
how far I have to go, how much time I have left to do it,
how much elevation I have climbed and how much more I'll
have to climb to reach my destination. And, if I'm hiking
with someone else, we might want to hike alone for a while
and meet at a specific time. So I always carry a watch.

For my JMT hike, I went a step farther and bought a
Suunto Vector watch. In addition to time, the Vector provides an alarm, a barometer (which aids in predicting
weather), an altimeter, a digital compass, and a digital
thermometer (provided you take it off your wrist for 15
minutes). The watch is waterproof, so you can even stick
it in a stream or lake if you want to know how cold the
water is. The altimeter provided useful information and
was fun to use; the elevation readings provided not only
current elevation, but also rate of ascent or descent, and
the elevation readings allowed me to know how much ele-

vation I had climbed (or descended) that day and how much more I had to go. This elevated my spirits at times when I was feeling tired, as it reminded me how far I already had come; I'd think, "Gee, I've already climbed 2,000 feet so the remaining 800 feet can't be so bad." Also, by cross-referencing your elevation with the map, you can determine where you are on the trail with great accuracy. Note, in using any altimeter, you need to adjust it at least once a day, to account for changing barometric pressure, when you reach points on the trail, such as mountain passes or lakes, where the elevation is known. So long as you do this, altimeters are pretty accurate.

I also carried music with me, for the first time ever in the backcountry, in the form of the Sony Walkman Memory Stick Audio Player. The audio player weighs just 1¼ ounces, the battery, which lasts 10 hours, weighs just ¾ ounce and the memory sticks are so light they don't even register on my electronic postal scale, which measures in increments of ⅛ ounce. For each section of the JMT, I took one battery and three memory sticks, each of which included two to three full CDs. For approximately 2½ ounces, including superlight headphones, I had music for a week. I didn't use it very often, as frequently I was hiking and talking with Jacobus or other hikers we'd meet on the trail. At other times, I just enjoyed silence. But sometimes Jacobus would want to sprint ahead, particularly on the hard climbs, and I'd put the headphones on, put in a memory stick with Marvin Gaye, Sam Cooke, or Stevie Ray Vaughn, and a hard climb would be transformed into a wonderful music experience. The miles and elevation would magically become easier. The music didn't distract from the wilderness at all because, instead of thinking of a million other things that might pass through my mind, the music actually enhanced my feelings of connection to nature. Listening to good music and observing nature both are highly spiritual experiences.

Things You Don't Need

It often amazes me what some people consider essential. *Backpacker* magazine once asked readers to identify "one piece of gear they never hit the trail without." The answers included hand pruners for helping with trail maintenance (noble, but heavy), popcorn popper, newspaper to barter with news-deprived backpackers, kite, nail polish "to keep my toes pretty," A flyswatter, telescoping marshmallow stick and Raisinettes to fool people into thinking he was identifying animals by tasting their droppings.

Many people carry a groundsheet in addition to a tent, supposedly to protect the tent floor and to use for sleeping out. In my opinion, carrying a groundsheet for these purposes is unnecessary. Good quality tents don't need groundsheets placed under their floor. When you want to sleep out, use the tent rain fly as your groundsheet and save 10 to 16 ounces.

I have seen backpackers carrying aluminum chairs, even chaise lounges, into the backcountry. If you think you need a chair, Therm-A-Rest makes a chair that uses a self-inflating air mattress as an insert. It's a bit of a hassle to get the inflated mattress into the chair sleeve, but once in, the chair works well and is very comfortable. But the chair weighs 11 ounces, exclusive of the air mattress. That's a lot less than an aluminum chair, and a lot more packable, as the sleeve rolls up compactly, but do you really need it? After carrying one for half of my JMT trip, my answer became, "No, it's not worth 11 ounces," and I began sitting on logs, rocks, and our bear canister, which doubles as a decent stool. My son, Jacobus, disagreed; he carried his Therm-a-Rest chair the full length of the JMT and used it every morning and evening.

Binoculars can be nice, particularly for watching animals, and good 10-power binoculars weighing as little as seven ounces can be found. But it's a luxury you don't use that often on the trail. We carried ours for 12 days, then sent them home at one of our resupply spots.

Like binoculars, GPS units are a nice luxury, and some, like the Garmin eTrex at 5½ ounces, are pretty light (but you also will need to carry a lot of extra batteries). A GPS unit will provide longitude and latitude information, which, when used in conjunction with a map, will tell you where you are, but they are completely unnecessary on the JMT. As noted earlier, the JMT is a well-marked trail, and with your Tom Harrison map, you are not going to get lost. A GPS also provides altitude information, but a Suunto watch will do the same at a lot less weight and will provide temperature, a clock, an alarm to wake you up in the morning, and barometric pressure information, as well.

Everyone loves a pillow. I once had a woman show up for a first date with a pillow under her arm, certainly an encouraging sign of what the possibilities would be that night. And there are some seductive little backpacking pillows out there, weighing in at just three to six ounces, beckoning you to favor a little luxury over backcountry simplicity. But that three to six ounces is weight you don't need. You always have extra clothing, a fleece or down jacket, perhaps, that can be rolled up or shoved into the hood of your sleeping bag and used as a pillow. Or, you can cram clothes into a stuff sack or Ziploc bag.

I normally don't carry games on a backpacking trip, but for the JMT, considering that we would be out for a month, we brought a miniature chess set and a deck of cards. Only once did we actually play a few hands of gin rummy; the rest of the time we had too many things to do or were just too tired to play cards or chess. So, I put cards and games in the luxury category.

Lastly, and this is by far the hardest one for me, is a book. I feel naked without reading material in my hand or back pocket (I once read 22 books on a three-week vacation). Naturally, I brought a book for each section of the JMT. I barely read one in the whole month. There is a lot to do that fills up the backpacking day, so there is not a lot of down time to sit and read. At night, I was just too tired to read. When we did have down time, I preferred to talk to Jacobus, look at the map and upcoming trail descriptions, or just look around and enjoy the sounds of nature—wind rushing through trees, a stream cascading nearby, birds or a marmot chirping, an owl hooting. In the city, we get our brains revved up and seem to need constant stimulation. In nature, we want to relax, listen more, and enjoy a new type of serenity not available in the city. A book, marvelous as it may be, can be a distraction to that serenity and opportunity to connect with nature. Leaving it at home saves you five to ten ounces and opens your mind to new possibilities.

Food

For breakfasts, Jacobus and I carried a small amount of

homemade granola, and a large amount of instant oat-meal. We carried more oatmeal than granola because the oatmeal is much lighter than granola and because, when heated and absorbed with water, it is a more filling meal. The instant oatmeal required just a few minutes to heat water and pour it on the oatmeal in our lexan bowls, a few minutes for it to sit in the bowls, and we had a completely satisfactory breakfast. For lunches, we brought crackers, cheese, salami, and turkey jerky (which we used both for lunch and a snack). This is not the lightest possible lunch, but we needed fat in our diet and we couldn't think of any-thing that would be lighter and as tasty. Cheese will easily last three to four days if you keep it in the bear canister at night, as the night temperatures are colder than a refriger-ator, then store it deep inside your pack during the day.

For dinners, we took freeze-dried food made by Mountain House, Alpine Aire, Backpacker's Pantry, and Natural High. For each dinner, we had an entrée, with portions for four for the two of us, a side dish of vegeta-bles, soup or potatoes and a dessert. We found the double portion of the entrée was sufficient to fill us up and after the first section of hiking we abandoned most of the side dishes and desserts. The entrees we took included "Chicken Gumbo," "Katmandu Curry," "Tuna with Noodles," "Chicken Stir Fry," "Honey-Lime Chicken," "Spicy Thai Chicken," "Lasagna," "Spaghetti" and "Pasta Roma." We tried to stay away from entrees with pork and sugar and gravitated toward pastas with tomato sauce. (I operate on the theory that anything with red sauce can't be bad.) Overall, we were satisfied with the tastiness of the food. Not exactly like eating at Chez Panisse, but not bad when you are tired and hungry. There wasn't a huge difference among the various freeze-dried food companies, but if we were forced to make a choice we'd probably say that the Mountain House dishes were the tastiest.

The net weight of the entrées was about five to six ounces per person, despite the fact we were consuming double portions, so this truly is the lightest way to eat cooked food on the trail. However, the freeze-dried food comes in bulky, heavy packaging, which I did not want to carry. I asked at several backpacking supply stores whether it was safe to remove the packaging and put the food in Ziploc plastic bags and couldn't get a definitive answer, so I called Alpine Aire Foods and talked with Don, the owner. He was extremely helpful and told me there was no problem taking the food out of the packaging, that the food might experience some degradation of flavor in 60 days, but it would not spoil or become unsafe to eat. With that reassurance, we removed all the packaging, put the dinners in Ziploc freezer bags (which Don recommended), labeled them on the outside and saved ourselves a lot of weight and bulk. The downside to freeze-dried food is that it is more expensive, but some companies sell it in bulk without expensive packaging. See, e.g., www.alpineairefoods.com. A less expensive alternative is making your own dehydrated food, which is time-consuming but not particularly difficult. Doing this gives you the option of taking almost any type of meal you want. Most of the freeze-dried food packages say all you need to do is add boiling water to the food and let it sit for five to ten minutes, but we found that at high elevations it is better to add the food to a pot of boiling water, then simmer for five minutes before letting it sit for five to ten minutes.

We also brought a lot of snacks, including Powerbars,

Clif bars, granola bars, fig bars, gorp for Jacobus (based on my experience 30 years ago in Colorado, I refused to touch any of it), fruit leather, almonds, and dried fruit. We found that snacks were important for keeping our blood sugar levels up and maintaining energy through the day.

Lastly, we found we did not eat as much as you might think. Despite burning 3,000–4,000 calories on the trail each day, we ate no more, and often less, than we eat sitting on our butts in the city. Maybe it was the endorphins kicking in, but whatever it was we generally ate less food than we carried and were not hungry.

The John Muir Trail

Theodore A. Solomons, a founding member of the Sierra Club, is given credit for conceiving a trail in 1884 following the crest of the Sierra Nevada. This later became the John Muir Trail. Solomons made at least three attempts to hike the crest of the Sierras, in 1894, 1895, and 1896, but never succeeded in getting farther south than Kings River Canyon. The conditions Solomons faced, however, were extremely difficult. There was no trail along the crest, and there was far more snow on the Sierra passes. One hundred years ago, even in September, many of the passes remained covered in snow. Despite Solomons' failure to establish a north-south route from Yosemite to Mt. Whitney, he succeeded in making several first ascents and in naming the Evolution group of peaks.

The John Muir Trail was named in 1915, when the California Legislature appropriated $10,000 for its construction, in honor of Muir, who had died in 1914, and his enormous contributions to the preservation of the Sierra Nevada. Prodded by state senator Arthur Breed, a Sierra Club member, in subsequent years the state made additional appropriations for construction of the trail. The route of the JMT was selected by California state engineer William F. McClure in consultation with the U.S. Forest Service and the Sierra Club, with most of the work being carried out by the Forest Service. Temporary routes west of the Sierra Crest were utilized until ways were found to cross certain passes, particularly Muir Pass, Mather Pass, and finally Foresters Pass, which was completed in 1931. [See, Francis P. Farquhar, *History of the Sierra Nevada*, 1969, University of California Press, for a more complete discussion of the history and exploration of the Sierra Nevada.]

John Muir was born in Scotland in 1838. He emigrated to the United States at age 11 and grew up on a farm in Wisconsin. Muir graduated from the University of Wisconsin in 1863 and went to work in a manufacturing plant, where he invented new pieces of equipment and became so valuable the owner of the company offered him half of the business as an inducement to stay. But Muir had suffered an accident on the job when a piece of metal flew into his eye and blinded him for several weeks. Muir pledged to himself that if he got his vision back he would leave work and see America. On recovering his sight, he left Wisconsin for an extended walk down the Mississippi to the Gulf and from the Gulf to Florida. Later, he walked to California, which remained his home until his death. Muir hiked extensively throughout the Sierras, making a number of first ascents along the Sierra crest, but it is unlikely he ever traveled the complete route of the current JMT.

Muir wrote about his travels in the Sierras for *Scribner's Monthly* and *Overland Monthly* magazines. His main works about the Sierras are *The Mountains of California* (1894), *Our National Parks* (1901), *My First*

Summer in the Sierra (1911), *The Yosemite* (1912), *Letters to a Friend* (1915), and *Studies in the Sierra* (1950, reprinted from magazine articles). Muir considered himself a poor writer and wrote mainly to publicize the beauty and value of the wildlands he was trying to save. But anyone who reads his nature writings will see he is poetic and beautifully descriptive. Reading—and re-reading—Muir is a joy no lover of nature should miss.

Muir is credited with being the first to explain that Yosemite Valley, and many Sierra valleys and land forms, were the result of glaciation, not the "convulsive" movement of the earth's crust, the theory that most geologists subscribed to at the time. Muir wrote: "In the beginning of a long glacial winter, the lofty Sierra seems to have consisted of one vast undulated wave, in which a thousand separate mountains, with their domes and spires, their innumerable canyons and lake basins, lay concealed. In the development of these, the Master Builder chose for a tool, not the earthquake nor lightning to rend asunder, not the stormy torrent nor eroding rain, but the tender snow-flowers, noiselessly falling through unnumbered seasons, the offspring of the sun and sea." [Muir, *Studies in the Sierra*] For his efforts and observations, Muir was called a "mere sheepherder, an ignoramus," by Professor Josiah Dwight Whitney, for whom Mt. Whitney is named. Whitney wrote, "A more absurd theory was never advanced than that by which it was sought to ascribe to glaciers the sawing out of these vertical walls and the rounding of the domes. This theory, based on entire ignorance of the whole subject, may be dropped without wasting any more time on it." [Whitney Survey, *The Yosemite Guide-Book*, 1869] Time and additional scientific studies proved Muir's observations and conclusions to be accurate, and Whitney the ignoramus.

In 1892, John Muir and 26 others founded the Sierra Club, "To explore, enjoy, and render accessible the mountain regions of the Pacific Coast; to publish authentic information concerning them; to enlist the support and cooperation of the people and the government in preserving the forests and other natural features of the Sierra Nevada." John Muir was elected the Sierra Club's first president, and he spent the rest of his life fighting to preserve the mountains he loved.

JOURNAL OF THE HIKE

Yosemite Valley to Tuolumne Meadows

Jacobus, Leon, and I decide it would be wise to use the first section of the JMT, from Yosemite Valley to Tuolumne Meadows, to test our physical condition and equipment and pick three days in June for the hike. We want to get an early start, so we stay overnight in the Valley at the Yosemite Lodge. The lodge is located near the base of Yosemite Falls, the highest waterfall in America and spectacular in June when it is full of water. Reservations in the Valley for lodges, tent camps, and campsites are greatly in demand in the summer, so you should call early for reservations (559/252-4848 for lodging); we are lucky to get a cancellation.

After breakfast at the lodge cafeteria the free Yosemite shuttle bus takes us to Happy Isles, entrance to the JMT. From the bus stop, it is a five-minute walk along the Merced River to the trailhead (4,035 feet), where I plan to take a photo of the first trail sign, which lists the miles to Mt. Whitney. Unfortunately, the beautiful old wooden trail sign had been washed away by the flood that inundated the valley in 1997. It had been replaced by an ugly metal sign donated by a Silicon Valley technology firm and neither identifies the trailhead as the start of the JMT nor references miles to Mt. Whitney. This proves to be one of my few disappointments on the JMT.

The first three miles are by far the most crowded of all the JMT. The hike to Vernal Falls is the most popular day hike from Yosemite Valley. In fact, the hike gets so much foot traffic, that the first mile is paved in asphalt. Nevertheless, and despite the hordes of day-hikers, many walking in tennis shoes and flip-flops, the hike is spectacular. It first ascends along the rushing Merced River, then reaches a beautiful wooden footbridge crossing the turbulent river and revealing dramatic Vernal Fall, famously photographed by Ansel Adams, the great chronicler of Yosemite scenery. Shortly after passing the bridge, the trail splits, with the Mist Trail following the river east toward Vernal Fall, and the JMT switch-backing steeply through dense forest up the south wall of the canyon until it reaches Clark Point (5,500 feet), where we stop to take in the great view of Vernal Fall, Nevada Fall, and Half Dome. For those who wish to hike the Mist Trail, it is shorter, steeper, and more dramatic, but in early summer can be wet and slippery from the mist of Vernal Fall blowing south on the trail. There are cables to hang on to near the top of the ascent to the fall, and often wonderful rainbows in the mist, so if you don't mind getting wet while dodging a lot of day-hikers, the Mist Trail is a worthwhile detour.

From Clark Point on the JMT, we decide to take a detour; Jacobus, Leon, and I leave our backpacks on the trail and descend on a well-used trail to Vernal Fall, then walk a couple hundred yards west to look over the edge of the fall. I've looked over this edge many times and each time

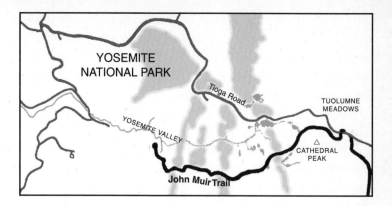

wondered about the people who have disregarded warnings about going beyond the fence and tried to jump across to one of the small islands in the river above the fall, only to slip on the slippery wet granite and be swept over the fall to their certain deaths on the rocks below. What went through their minds as they went over the edge and realized they had only seconds to live? My fantasy has been to swim in beautiful Emerald Pool a quarter-mile above the fall, but the thought of being swept into the river and over the fall has prevented me from swimming there for the 50 years I've been hiking in Yosemite.

After snacking up at Vernal Fall, we walk back to our packs and continue our hike to the top of Nevada Fall (6,000'). At the top, off come our boots and socks so we can dangle our feet in the river while eating a relaxed lunch. We share the gorgeous California weather in the company of many backpackers, most of whom are doing two- to three- day hikes into Little Yosemite Valley and/or to Merced Lake. After lunch, it's a mile to our day's destination, Little Yosemite Valley. Little Yosemite Valley is notorious for bears and it is easy to see why. The place is crowded with backpackers camping on nearly every available piece of flat ground, many of whom are ignoring the bear boxes the National Park Service has provided. On a past trip into Little Yosemite Valley, I once followed a very large brown bear in the middle of the day, while most campers were taking day hikes or swimming in the river. The bear ambled around the campground just like it was a supermarket, removing food from tents, eating food left outside, and just having the most wonderful time. On another trip, before the NPS installed bear boxes, I hung the food bags 20 feet high on a cable installed by the NPS. Despite the fact that the tent was pitched right underneath the hanging food bags, in the morning the bags were gone. The bears not only had gotten bags that were hung perfectly, according to NPS instructions, but they had done so without waking me up and giving me a chance to try to scare them off. Now the NPS requires backpackers to store food in bear boxes, which are provided in some highly used campsites, or in their own bear canisters. This rule not only protects backpackers' food, but more importantly, it also protects bears and other scavenging animals from becoming dependent on human food.

After fixing an early dinner, we put all our food in a nearby bear box, converse with two backpackers who pitch their tent no more than 15 feet from ours, listen to how they plan to use their spray canisters of Mace on any bear with the audacity to visit them, then bed down in the fading light. No sooner have we climbed into our sleeping bags than someone in the distance starts yelling and banging pots. This can mean only one thing: a bear has shown up in camp to pillage food. As the night proceeds, the yelling and pot banging happens every few minutes. Then, around 10 p.m., our next-door neighbors begin yelling and rustling around. I stick my head out of the tent to see what's going on, and there are our two neighbors leaning out of their tent, each holding a can of Mace. They explain that a bear came to their open tent door, they Maced it, and it ran away. I'm not sure if this is their imagination running amok, but I go back to sleep. With no food or cosmetics in our tent, there is no reason for us to fear bears.

If there were an extra day, I would want to detour 3½ miles up the Merced Lake trail to Bunnel Cascades, a fabulous 100-foot-long waterslide on smooth granite into a large pool of water, but we don't have the time. So the next day we begin a steep ascent on the north side of the canyon, heading north toward Sunrise High Sierra Camp. The sun is hot, part of the trail is deep sand, and the boys are moving a lot faster than I am. A mile and a half up the trail, we pass a junction (7,000 feet) with the trail to Half Dome—a four-mile round-trip to the top of Half Dome (8,835feet) with fabulous views of Yosemite Valley. I continue to trudge up the switch-backing trail, thinking my pack is light for this three-day trip. I'll need to get stronger for the heavier packs we'll be carrying 200+ miles from Tuolumne Meadows to Whitney Portal.

I'm hiking with a Gregory backpack that I've used for nearly 15 years, one of the original internal-frame packs. It's the best pack I've ever owned, and I'm happy with it, but I ask Leon and Jacobus about trying their packs. Jacobus is carrying a Mountainsmith pack—I try it on, walk for a half-mile with it, and find it no improvement over my old Gregory. Leon has a new Dana Design Terraplane pack. After carrying it a mile or so, it's clear that the Dana is much more stable than my Gregory, which tends to sway. The Dana pack has many more adjustments than the Gregory, permitting a closer fit and more of a feeling that the pack is integrated with the body, plus it has more volume, which will be useful on the JMT. It is a much more sophisticated pack and clearly superior to my Gregory, but the thought of giving up my beloved old friend bothers me. I decide to buy a Dana pack after returning home, and will send the Gregory out to my house in Utah for canyoneering trips. Jacobus, hearing my praise of the Dana, tries it and likes it as much as I do. I think we'll all soon be carrying the same packs.

We pass Sunrise camp (9,300 feet) late in the afternoon, then camp on a bench above Long Meadow, with good views east toward Tuolumne Meadows, Cathedral Peak, and the Unicorn, and enjoy the sunset in the west. I'm very tired, though it's satisfying to hike 11 miles and climb more than 3,000 feet. But Jacobus advises, "You'll have to be in better condition for the long hike." Tomorrow, we'll hike more miles, but only about 1,000 feet of elevation gain, so I console myself with the knowledge that the hardest part of this section of the trail is past. In September I will have a better pack and be in better shape.

The next day, there's a descent to beautiful Long Meadow, still very soggy but full of wildflowers, and climb along the side of Tresidder Peak to Cathedral Pass (9,700 feet). From here, the trail descends to the west end of Tuolumne Meadows, then turns east, paralleling Highway 120, until it reaches the Tuolumne Meadows Campground (8,600 feet) and the Lyell Fork of the Tuolumne River. From this point, and for the next 200 miles, the JMT will head generally south.

The three of us set our packs alongside the road heading west, stick out our thumbs, and within 45 minutes have a ride back to our car, which is waiting in Yosemite Valley. I'm satisfied with our performance on this section and know that our weakest link—me—will be stronger in September.

Tuolumne Meadows to Reds Meadow

Day 1

It's a late night making final adjustments to my gear and saying "goodbye" to Jeanine. Then I am awakened by the phone ringing. It is Clara from Muir Trail Ranch saying it is OK to land a helicopter in the meadow by the Ranch with Jeanine and Jacobus' girlfriend, Heather. Before I can get out of the house, there are more phone calls from my architect, lawyers in my National Missile Defense system lawsuit, and friends saying goodbye. As a result, we don't depart until 11:30 a.m.

Jacobus and I drive to Tuolumne Meadows with our friend Catie, who will then take the car back home, since we can't leave it in Yosemite for a month. Along the way, we get a phone call from Leon in Paris, telling us of his new girlfriend and his exploits in photography, then wishing us the best on the hike. I will miss Leon, his love of communication, and his cheery disposition.

We arrive at the Tuolumne Meadows Campground and unload our packs from the car, have Catie take a few photos of us, both give her big hugs, then throw on our packs, wave a last goodbye, and head for the trail on the south side of the campground. After stopping at the trailhead sign for an obligatory photo, we begin the hike at 4:20 p.m. on a glorious, warm Yosemite day under blue skies. I am exhilarated, having dreamed of hiking the entire JMT nearly all my life. Now I'm actually on the trail doing it—and with Jacobus.

Walking along the meandering Lyell Fork of the Tuolumne River, with its gentle cascades over smooth granite and quiet blue-green pools of water, we talk excitedly of the trail and adventures ahead. After continuing a couple of miles, we encounter a backpacker from Canada, who asks where we are headed. "The end of the trail," I tell him. He says, "You mean the whole John Muir Trail? I've wanted to do that all my life." I reply, "You're still young, but I've been thinking of doing this for 40 years and now I'm doing it!" We walk with him, talking for 30 to 40 minutes. A big advocate of lightpacking, he claims to have his basic equipment reduced to 21 pounds, plus food. He also hikes with lightweight running shoes, claiming never to have had foot problems on the trail. "A pound on your feet is equal to five pounds on your back," he advises.

We spot a gorgeous site next to the river, so Jacobus and I bid him adieu and set up camp. The Stephenson Warmlite tent goes up easily, and all our gear fits inside with a lot of room to spare. Jacobus sets up the stove and cooks some Alpine Aire Katmandu Curry, which we rate, "not bad." The "four portions" turn out to be just right for the two of us, with no need to cook the side dish of potatoes gratin or dessert. We enjoy a beautiful sunset, listening to the nearby river, then darkness descends quickly and the Milky Way appears sparkling brightly. Jacobus identifies a prominent orange object on the horizon as Mars. We stay up late talking, then crawl into the tent for the night.

Day 2

At 8 a.m., just as the sun comes over the east ridge and hits the tent, we awake. Frost is still on the roof of the tent, but the sun warms us quickly and dries the tent. Jacobus heats water for oatmeal, then strips naked and takes a swim in the beautiful blue-green waters of the Lyell Fork, which he shares with John Muir's favorite bird, the Water Ouzel—or, as Jacobus reminds me, the American Dipper, its formal name. The weather is absolutely perfect—warm sun, blue skies, and a faint hint of a breeze. Oh, to have such weather for the whole trip.

The weather stays like this all day as we walk alongside the river, stopping at lunch for a nap and for me to jump in the water. Then we climb some steep switchbacks up to 9,650 feet, where the trail crosses the Lyell Fork on a bridge. We camp downstream in a delightful campsite overlooking the bridge, full of great camp furniture. The walk today has been gorgeous, with big meadows and the Lyell Fork on our left (east) and Donohue Peak and Mt. Lyell, at 13,144 feet the highest peak in Yosemite, looming ahead, alerting us to the elevation climb in front of us. For me, the climb up the switchbacks was enhanced by James Taylor, Eric Clapton, and Ry Cooder playing on my new Sony Walkman Memory Stick—2½ ounces, including battery and headphones. But there's only one 10-hour battery to last until we get to Red's Meadows in five days.

Top: Devil's Postpile (page 106)
Bottom: South of Reds Meadow and Devil's Postpile (page 112)

Top: Squaw Lake below Silver Pass (page 117)
Bottom: Sunset at Squaw Lake (page 117)

Top: Top of Silver Pass (page 118)
Bottom: View north from Silver Pass (page 118)

Top: Muir Trail Ranch (page 123)
Bottom: Cascade on Evolution Creek (Page 127)

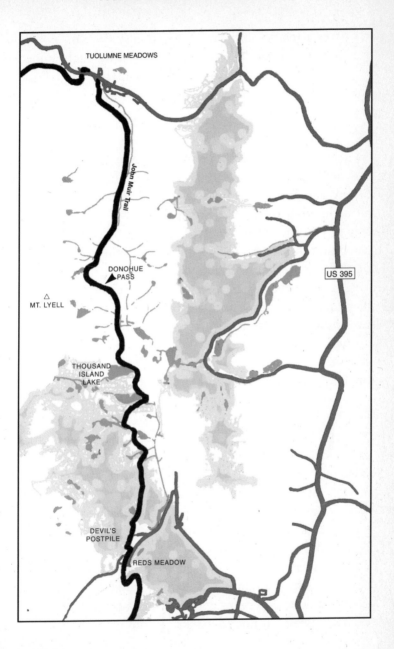

After a relaxed dinner, it was an easy decision not to put up the tent and instead bed down for the night under a crystal sky, listening to the sounds of the Lyell Fork steeply cascading nearby.

Day 3

Awake at 7:45 a.m. after a good sleep, we linger at breakfast talking, then start hiking at 10:30. The campsite had been wonderful—listening to the river cascades next to us all night—but to enjoy it, we stopped two miles and 500 feet of elevation gain short of our intended camp. We'll catch up today by hiking 11 miles and climbing two passes, the first serious hiking day.

An hour of climbing takes us to an absolutely spectacular tarn alongside a meadow at 10,200 feet, with Mt. Lyell and the Mt. Lyell glacier accentuating the background. The water in the tarn is a thousand subtle shades of blue and green, inviting us to jump in, but the length of the hike today and our late start do not permit the luxury of a swim, so we start up the trail toward Donohue Pass (11,056 feet). Halfway up, we encounter two backpackers from Oklahoma taking a break alongside another gorgeous tarn with Mt. Lyell in the background, a scene reminiscent of the cover of the Sierra Club format book on the Sierras titled *Gentle Wilderness,* which was taken in Center Basin, 100+ miles south of here. These two hikers had started their trip at Giant Forest, in Kings Canyon National Park, hiked the High Sierra Trail (a 72-mile west–east lateral), then headed north when they crossed the JMT, taking a number of detours along the way. In all, they had done 220 miles with only one resupply and were each carrying 70-pound packs. I comment, "That's an awful lot of weight to carry," and the hiker with the pony-tail says, "Yes it is, but it got me in shape, caused me to burn off a lot of fat, and made me give up smoking." That sounds like a fair trade to me, but I'm happy with my 42-pound pack; days of carrying 50- to 60-pound packs are just a distant memory.

We have a nice chat with these two young men about their hike and about Oklahoma. I ask them, "Why would anyone want to live in Oklahoma?" The ponytail replies, "Why would anyone want to live in the Midwest? I left Oklahoma and now live in Oregon." I ask them, "What did you think of Forester Pass?" and the ponytail says, "That's the pass that never ends; it just goes on and on and on." I ask them, "Of all the places you've seen in the last month, what is your favorite spot?" They both point to the tarn we're standing next to and Mt. Lyell in the background, and the ponytail says, "This is as good as anything." Without having walked as far as they, I have to agree; such a beautiful scene.

After saying farewell, it is on to the top of Donohue Pass, officially leaving Yosemite NP and entering the Ansel Adams Wilderness. At the top of the pass, we meet a middle-aged couple from England who are hiking the JMT in 20 days, doing 16 miles today. For a time, we keep pace with them, alternatively passing and being passed, until they pass us at the top of Island Pass (10,250 feet) and are gone, never to be seen again. The four-mile section between Donohue Pass and Island Pass is unique, the only part of the JMT that is east of the Sierra Crest. More important, it is a section affording spectacular views of the Ritter Range and the spires of the Minarets. This area is chock full of lakes and is bisected by the Middle Fork of the San Joaquin River. It's a favorite area of mine, for its natural beauty, proximity to the San Francisco Bay Area, abundance of three- to five-day loops, and the fall colors of aspens along the San Joaquin River and in the lake canyons. But it is popular, and the lakes attract backpackers.

Rather than camp at the largest and most popular of the Minaret area lakes, Thousand Island Lake, Jacobus and I stop at the top of Island Pass and find a small lake with good campsites as well as great views of Banner Peak (12,936 feet) and parts of the Ritter Range. We're the only campers at this great spot. Once camp is set up, Jacobus says, "Congratulations on completing our first hard day." Great to hear.

Day 4

Since our campsite is on the top of a pass, the sun hits us early. We're up at 7:30 a.m. and on the trail at 10. It's a nice walk down to Thousand Island Lake (9,833 feet), where we take a break and some photos of the spectacular lake with Banner Peak on the west end. Next, on to Ruby Lake and several unnamed lakes, before descending to Garnet Lake (9,678 feet), with Banner Peak and Mt. Ritter (13,143 feet) in the background. A granite slab on the east end of Garnet Lake provides a stop for lunch to enjoy the big views. We bask in the hot sun while getting whipped by the strong wind coming off the lake. We'd like to swim in Garnet, but the wind is discouraging, so our best hope is for a small lake or stream on the way to Shadow Lake.

The trail leads around the south shore before leaving Garnet and climbing steeply to a saddle that then descends to Shadow Creek. On the descent, we meet a young couple on their honeymoon, she from Palo Alto and he from Dublin, Ireland. She asks our destination, and when we tell her "Mt. Whitney," she gets very excited and says, "I've hiked the John Muir Trail twice, once when I was 11 and again when I was 14." I say, "Didn't your dad have to beat you with a stick to get you to hike that far?" "No, not at all," she says, "He just said, 'Honey, we're going on a hike and we went.'" Her father, a professor at Stanford, is still an avid hiker at 75. She says she wants to hike the JMT a third time—with her new husband. I ask him what he thinks about that idea. "It sounds like a great idea to me," he says.

The long descent to Shadow Creek is dry, and I am at the end of my water supply. But at Shadow Creek the reward is a great swimming hole just beneath a ten-foot cascade. We both whip off our boots and clothes and jump in. The water temperature is not 82 degrees, as I had requested, but warm enough to stay in for quite awhile and return to the trail completely refreshed and ready for the 700-foot climb to Rosalie Lake (9,350 feet).

On the way to Rosalie Lake, we meet The Purple Hat Man, a middle-aged backpacker wearing a bright purple, floppy hat. He hands me a business card:

PACK TOO HEAVY?

Let Purple Hat show you how he hiked for 30 days with a 30-pound pack, carrying all of his food, or how he hiked the John Muir Trail in 13 days with a 20-pound pack, also carrying all of his food. $25 for either report, or $45 for both! (559) 251-1249.

Purple Hat is, indeed, carrying a very small pack, so we ask him how much food he is carrying. "Only 800 calories a day, plus my own fat," he replies. I look at his sagging, flabby midsection, which he explains was achieved as a result of concentrated loading of carbohydrates, fat, sugar, and chocolate before his trip, plus "beer blasting." "So the fat of your belly is part of your food supply?" I ask. "Absolutely," Purple Hat says. "Well, then, aren't you really carrying a 40-pound pack—20 on your back and an extra 20 on your stomach?" Purple Hat laughs, looks at our stomachs and adds, "This system might not work very well for you guys."

Purple Hat has hiked the JMT twice before—once in 13 days and again in 45. I ask him which he enjoyed better. "They were different," he says. "The 13-day trip was all hiking, no time for anything else. The 45-day trip gave me time to explore, to fish, to swim. It was very relaxing." I note to Jacobus that our trip, 29 days, is exactly the midpoint of Purple Hat's fast and relaxing JMT hikes.

Purple Hat isn't a particularly fast hiker—we both pass him up on the climb to Rosalie Lake—but he starts early in the morning, often 6:30 or 7 a.m., and hikes late. Today, he plans to hike until 9 or 10 p.m. to get to Reds Meadow, despite the fact that it will be dark by 8 p.m.. He also is very disciplined. He eats no lunch and walks for exactly 48 minutes, then takes a 12-minute break, no more, for water and snacks. He has an alarm on his Casio which beeps every 12 minutes to remind him to drink water. The tortoise can get there first, I guess. We find a nice campsite at Rosalie Lake near the trail, and 20 minutes later, Purple Hat appears. We wish him the best and off he goes, chugging along at his own pace, burning fat and handing out "Purple Hat" cards.

After completing the JMT, I call Purple Hat to see how he did on his hike and to order his report on his 13-day JMT hike. I have a nice conversation with him, send him $25, and he sends me a personal letter with "Purple Hat: adventurer, big wall climber, lake swimmer, solo hiker, wilderness photographer, writer" on the top of the page. His 51-page report ("The Ultimate John Muir Trail Experience!"), with Purple Hat on the cover skinning-dipping in a hot springs (wearing a purple hat, of course), along with an 8" x 10" glossy photograph of Garnet Lake, a greeting card with a photograph of "California Coneflowers," Membership Card #10,003 in the "Purple Hat Adventure Travel Club" (I'd be real surprised if I was the 10,003rd member; more likely, I'm the third member), a refrigerator magnet that says, "How can I be out of money? I still have checks," and a copy of "Purple Hat's Catalogue" describing Purple Hat books, Purple Hat lightweight backpacking gear, Purple Hat's short stories ($1.25 each and six for $6), Purple Hat Sierra Wilderness Photographs, Purple Hat Sierra Wilderness Photograph Greeting Card Sets, Purple Hat Sierra Wilderness Photograph T-Shirts, Purple Hat Sierra Wilderness Photograph Magnets, and a list of products "From the Other Side of My Brain." These include Osama Dead Laden and Saddam Hussein T-Shirts (available in red, white or blue), sets of Sonora Cigar right- and left-handed lighters in Hot Pink, Purple, and assorted colors, and a list described at the top as "Very Funny Magnets." In case anyone misses the "Very Funny" description, at the bottom of the list of magnets, Purple Hat adds, "Each magnet has the above saying with an image or images that intensifies the joke and all are very funny." Samples of "Other Brain" magnet humor include:

CAT MISSING? CHECK UNDER MY TIRES!

I LOVE CATS; THEY TASTE JUST LIKE CHICKEN.

SO MANY CATS, SO FEW RECIPES!

HAND OVER THE CHOCOLATE AND NOBODY GETS HURT!

WILL WORK FOR CHOCOLATE.

WORK IS FOR PEOPLE WHO CAN'T GOLF.

I'M NOT SUFFERING FROM INSANITY; I'M ENJOYING IT.

YOU'RE JUST JEALOUS BECAUSE YOU DON'T HEAR THE VOICES.

NOT ALL WHO WANDER ARE LOST.

ON TIME IS WHEN I GET THERE.

I don't know about the cats, but the jokes about chocolate seem to be serious. I read his report and he appears to be a full-blown, unrepentant chocoholic. An example of a Purple Hat chocolate attack on a prior JMT hike:

Of course, you know that "it is never too early to eat chocolate!" While I generally tried—to not start eating chocolate until lunch time—there was one morning where the night had gone badly, and the only way to get the day off to a good start was to eat chocolate. First I just was going to have a few pieces, then just the M & Ms.

Then even the fake mini M & Ms. Gripped with a full blown chocolate attack, I even committed a cardinal sin: I opened up the next day's lunch and started on its chocolate! I obviously hadn't brought enough chocolate. When I got to VVR

[Vermillion Valley Resort] I smartly bought several bags of M & Ms to create "an emergency" supply to protect me just from such tough nights as I've described.

How could I have foreseen, however, that within two hours of having created my emergency supply, I would have another chocolate emergency causing me to consume my supply!

—"The Ultimate John Muir Trail Experience!"

Purple Hat definitely has a style of his own, and, despite his eccentricities, I respect him. He's living life on his own terms, out in the backcountry enjoying the same things that I consider so important, and he's hiked the JMT three times to my one. His report describes an approach to hiking the JMT that many will prefer to avoid, but it contains useful ideas and some good intended, as well as unintended, humor that is more than worth $25— plus, you could join the Purple Hat Adventure Travel Club, go "beer blasting" before a trip, or maybe even share a bag of M & Ms with him.

Day 5

We both sleep 10½ hours and awaken at 8 a.m. More sleep seems necessary on the JMT than at home, probably the effect of the clean air and exercise.

Before the trip, my biggest concern had been blisters, but so far I've had no foot problems and my boots feel fine. However, the hipbelt of my pack has caused some serious welts and abrasions. The pack keeps sliding down my back, putting more tension and weight on the front of my hipbones, and the flesh is giving out. Yesterday, I put moleskin on the welts, and that only seemed to make things worse. The moleskin made the welts even hotter and kept the damaged skin wet, preventing healing. In pain, I do little more than continue to shift the weight of the pack as I walk, hoping to find a spot on my hips where the pack feels comfortable.

Leaving Rosalie Lake, we hike a short way to Gladys Lake, a shallow lake with a nice sandy beach, and pass Trinity Lakes, a series of shallow meadow lakelets. Then it is a 2,000-foot descent to the entrance to Devils Postpile National Monument, where we cross the Middle Fork of the San Joaquin River on a new (1996) steel bridge. I decide on the "traditional" JMT route through Devils Postpile over the "current" JMT route, which bypasses the Postpile. We stop at Devils Postpile to read the exhibit displays and look at the fascinating basalt rock formations, then we begin a climb to Reds Meadow Resort, where we will be resupplied and stay the night in a cabin.

I'm not feeling well—a sore throat, drippy nose, and weak feeling. I caught a cold the day before swimming in Shadow Creek for too long and getting chilled, then eating a late dinner in the cold. I have not brought enough warm clothes and hope to supplement my wardrobe, or at least get a warmer knit hat, at Reds Meadow Store, or catch a shuttle into Mammoth Lakes, where outdoor supply stores are plentiful.

Arriving at Reds Meadow Store around 4 p.m., we get the key to our cabin and request our resupply boxes. They look in the back and can't find anything. I call home, speak with my assistant, Laurie, ask what address our supplies were mailed to, and she tells me they were sent to Bob Tanner, owner of Reds Meadow Store and Resort at his business address in Mammoth Lakes. I go inside the store to ask if Bob Tanner is around and am told that Tanner is outside getting ready to leave for the day. I sprint out to the parking lot and confront Tanner just as he is about to drive away. "Have you received any boxes for me?" I ask. He casually replies, "Oh, I have a bunch of boxes in the back of the truck." It turns out he's been carrying our two boxes, along with resupply boxes for other backpackers, in the back of his truck for several days without mentioning this to anyone. This kind of behavior turns out to be typical of the lackadaisical attitude at Reds Meadow Resort.

We load our packs and supply boxes in our dingy cabin at the "resort," take showers to get the trail grime off, then go to the Reds Meadow Resort Café only to be told that dinner is not available because we didn't order it by 3 p.m. When I made cabin reservations a month ago, no one said dinner had to be ordered in advance. We order off the lunch menu—cheeseburgers, salad and fries and what turns out to be the worst "homemade" peach pie I've ever eaten—then go back to the cabin to sort our new supplies for the hike tomorrow. Added to this, I have big red welts on the front of both hips, some of which have broken open and bled. If my hips get any worse, I won't be able to continue. Jacobus decides that the trouble I'm having with the hipbelt is that my pack is misadjusted, so he removes the metal stay in the back of the pack and bends it to better fit the small of my back and rest on the top of my butt, thus taking pressure off the front hips. Most likely, the stay was bent and the pack came out of adjustment as the result of my sitting on it. The pack seems to feel better, but only hiking on the trail with a full load will tell me for sure if the problem has been solved. In any case, I'm impressed with Jacobus' ability to refit the pack.

Before going to sleep, I load up on some immune boosters and vitamin C, but find Aconitum, the most appropriate homeopathic remedy, missing from our first-aid kit. If I had Aconitum, my cold would be history by morning, but without it, I'm not so sure the immune boosters and C will do the job.

Reds Meadow to Muir Trail Ranch

Day 6

After sleeping 11 hours, Jacobus and I shower (our last on the JMT), then re-sort our new supplies. On this section, we don't need as much food. We've been eating our main courses (four portions for the two of us), but not the side dishes or desserts, and only about half of our lunch supplies. For the rest of the JMT, we can carry less food and won't have a problem fitting it into the two bear canisters.

Before leaving for breakfast, I mention to Jacobus that maybe we should take a layover day in Mammoth Lakes, 10 miles away. Still not feeling well, I would like to track down some Aconitum in Mammoth, and my hips could use a day's rest without a hipbelt squeezing them. Also, I hope to buy a warm hat and some long underwear. Jacobus is not happy about getting off the trail for a day and the issue is unresolved as we walk over to the café for breakfast.

Outside the café, we encounter two JMT hikers, Amy and Rob Nangle, from Ashland, Oregon, whom we had met earlier on the trail. Both look very distressed. They have decided to stay in Mammoth overnight "because of what happened this morning." I ask, "What happened this morning?" "Oh, my god, haven't you heard?" Amy exclaims. "Two planes were hijacked by terrorists and then crashed into the World Trade Center. Both towers have collapsed and 40,000 people may be dead." I think she must be kidding, but the expression on her face tells me she isn't. This really happened; it isn't science fiction or a Hollywood movie. I say to Jacobus, "This cinches it. We'll take a shuttle into Mammoth, rent a motel room, and watch the news, rest, buy some warm clothes, and try to find some Aconitum."

After ordering breakfast, Jacobus and I listen to radio accounts of the tragedy; the radio reception is scratchy and most of the coverage is about what Fresno is doing in response to the terrorist attack. I'm not much interested in listening to the Fresno mayor and am anxious to get to Mammoth to get some real news. After a breakfast of eggs and bacon, we quickly pack our new supplies into our backpacks and our excess supplies into a shipping box to be sent home. Randy's Shuttle Service provides an easy ride to the Shiloh Inn in Mammoth Lakes. Jacobus and I get a room, immediately flip on the TV and begin watching the incredible coverage of the terrorist attack.

Jacobus and I watch TV for several hours, then go out for lunch and shopping for some warm clothes and Aconitum. Once back in the room, we watch more TV, read two days of USA Today and the Los Angeles Times, call home, and call friends in New York to make sure they are alright. Amazingly, my niece, Unmi, is in New York City with my filmmaker friend, Vivi, and they watched the World Trade Center buildings disintegrate from a balcony no more than a mile away, getting dust all over

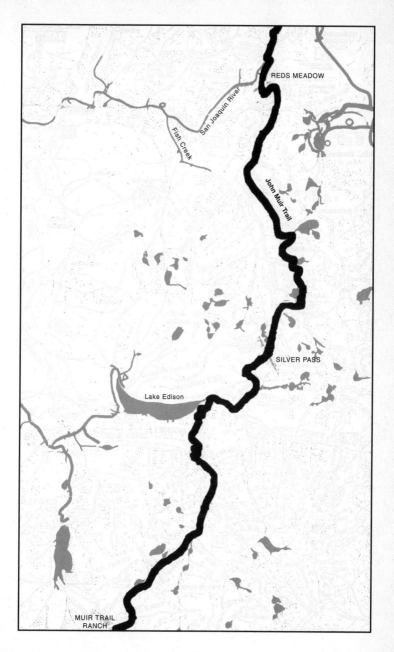

themselves. Unmi is so shaken by the experience, she and Vivi rent a car and immediately drive back to Unmi's home in Northampton, Massachusetts.

The TV is kept on, then I go to bed for what turns out to be a fitful night of sleep. It's not possible to escape the horrors of the world—even on the JMT.

Day 7

Jacobus and I wake to more nonstop coverage of "The Attack on America," then go to eat. I order "The Lumberjack Breakfast," which includes scrambled eggs, toast, hash browns, pancakes, and six slices of bacon. I'm determined to get some fat in my diet. I pick up two newspapers and read every story about the attack, and, as a consequence, we don't get back to Reds Meadow Resort and the trail until 12:45 p.m.

At least we thought we were on the JMT. We follow two signs at Reds Meadow Resort pointed to "JMT South." But, as we discover, both signs are inaccurate and point to an old, abandoned route of the JMT that is longer and steeper than the current route. I wonder how many other hikers have been misled by their inaccurate trail signs.

Back on the JMT, and, despite hiking steeply uphill in deep sand through a recent burn forest, we're both glad not to be glued to a TV watching the same terrible photos, listening to the same terrible story, glad just to be hiking again. Before getting on the trail, Jacobus says, "Dad, let me take some of the pressure off your hips by carrying some of your weight," so I give him a couple of dense, heavy items. My son the Sherpa—what a wonderful, compassionate hiking companion.

The Aconitum has knocked out my cold overnight.

Jacobus' pack readjustment, the rest day without a pack, and less weight, seems to have helped my hips. Jacobus also bought some gauze pads in town, which I tape over my hip bones and they help, too. It will take awhile to heal, but I'm going to be OK.

Despite the late start and the extra distance, we hike 8.1 miles in less than four hours and arrive at our camp at Deer Creek at a reasonable hour. Across the creek, we spot two backpackers who have a fire going and join them for dinner and conversation. They are both from Reno, in their 60s and have been backpacking all their lives. One of them has a satellite phone and I'm tempted to borrow it to call home, but having spoken with Jeanine five times in the past 24 hours, it's better just to enjoy the campfire and the company of these two fine gentlemen.

Day 8

Last night was the coldest night yet and tested the limit of my 15-degree sleeping bag, but Jacobus says he was OK. The morning also is cold, but as soon as the sun comes over the ridge and filters through the forest it warms up quickly. I go down to the creek to pump water for breakfast and encounter an average-size JMT hiker carrying the largest pack I've ever seen. When asked what it weighs, he says "80 pounds." "What could you possibly be carrying that would add up to 80 pounds?" "Well, I like to be comfortable, so I have a station-wagon-size Thermorest Luxury Edition, full-length air mattress that weighs five pounds, a bottle of Kahlua, and a bottle of Caymus Chardonnay, among other things. We also eat a lot of food and none of it is the light-weight stuff. We just went to the grocery store and bought whatever looked good. It is good, but the stuff is heavy," he says. His two hiking partners catch up, and their packs are just as big, plus all three are carrying some extra pounds around their waists. After talking to them, I'm convinced they're having a great time. If they have the ability to carry 80 pounds and still have fun, more power to them. We've now met JMT hikers carrying packs ranging from 20 to 80 pounds. Before leaving camp, our neighbors walk over and offer their satellite phone to us. A nice gesture, but we gracefully decline.

The hike is a steady climb on the south side of the mountains, with great views to the west of Cascade Valley 2,000' below with its large meadows, Fish Creek, and, according to our map, a hot springs, and to the south the Silver Divide. Cascade Valley is a place to explore on a future trip. Jacobus and I round the side of the mountain and drop 1,000 feet to Duck Creek, meeting a 22-year-old woman from San Luis Obispo hiking with her horse south to north. She has been walking and riding for the last five months and will finish the California portion of the Pacific Crest Trail as soon as she reaches Yosemite Valley, just a week away. She has had the greatest time of her life and is absolutely radiant with the joy of living in the wilderness. I hope she writes a book someday. We talk with her for a half-hour, then climb to exquisite Purple Lake (9,000 feet), where we meet a father and his two sons, 18 and 20, hiking the JMT south to north. Just short of Purple Lake and our next encounter, a young man from Colorado who is hiking the JMT. He tells us he just finished hiking the 500-mile-long Colorado Trail, which meanders from Denver to Durango, and will be going hiking in the Four Corners area as soon as he finishes the JMT—which won't be long, as he is hiking 17 miles a day.

We're meeting fewer hikers on this stretch of the JMT, and those hikers are all doing the JMT. This young man hikes for awhile with Jacobus and tells him that he had been at Reds Meadow the day before and called one of his buddies to tell him excitedly that he had just seen two bears devouring a deer carcass, when his buddy said, "Have you heard about the World Trade Center?" All of a sudden, the bear story wasn't so exciting.

Our next camp is a quarter of a mile below Purple Lake, since camping on the lake is not permitted, alongside cascading Purple Creek. A walk back to the lake, Jacobus takes a swim and I write in my waterproof journal. At the lake, we run into our first ranger, a young woman who has camped at Purple Lake all summer. In every two-week cycle, she spends nine days in the backcountry, then hikes out and spends one day in the office and has four days off, then hikes back to Purple Lake. She says last year it snowed on September 1 and then not until October 9. We're hoping that weather pattern repeats itself this year, as we plan to be off the JMT on October 4. So far the weather has been perfect—sunny, high-60s to mid-70s, dry, light breezes, crystal clear cloudless skies.

Day 9

Today, Jacobus and I take one of the most beautiful hikes. We leave Purple Lake and climb a 700-foot ridge, then descend to Lake Virginia (10,335 feet), a spectacular alpine lake with long, sandy beaches surrounded by 12,000-foot rock walls on the north and views of the Silver Divide to the south. The lake is so beautiful and the weather so fine that we linger on the edge of the lake for an hour. This lake is on my return list.

From Lake Virginia, we climb southeastward, take in views of the Silver Divide, McGee Pass, and Cascade Valley, then descend on switchbacks to Tully Hole and lovely Fish Creek, which meanders the length of Cascade Valley. On the hike down, Jacobus tells me about his favorite class and professor at the University of Oregon and his ideas about metaphysics; I didn't expect to be talking metaphysics, but we have a great conversation. At the bottom of the switchbacks we walk along Fish Creek for a mile, then find a great lunch spot next to the creek overlooking a stretch of deep green, quiet water, followed below by dashing cascades. It's a feast of salami, cheese and crackers. The spot is so idyllic, we don't want to leave, but there's still a 1,300-foot climb to Squaw Lake. So down the trail to a steel footbridge (9,100 feet) and a junction with the Cascade Valley Trail. Both of us would like to have an extra couple of days to explore Cascade Valley, but the JMT beckons so we cross the bridge, lingering to watch the cascades, then head toward Squaw Lake. It's uphill all the way, but Jacobus and I continue talking nonstop for two hours and the climb seems to require no effort.

Getting to Squaw Lake (10,300 feet) at 5 p.m., we locate the most perfect spot for a campsite, as the whole basin is ours, and take a quick swim in the lake. The camp is in a large, park-like, alpine basin, with grass underfoot, surrounded by dramatic rock-walls on three sides. Our campsite is exposed, but there is no wind and the weather is great. We have had nothing but great campsites up to this point, but Jacobus says this is the best yet. I agree.

At dinner, Jacobus and I watch every moment of the alpenglow on the eastern rocks; the show of light on the rock-wall makes it easy to understand why John Muir called the Sierra Nevada "the Range of Light." As the alpenglow leaves the eastern walls, we turn to watch the sunset on the distant horizon, squeezing every color shade out of it until the sky is dark and stars are glistening, then wait for the moon to rise and light up the whole basin. We haven't missed any part of this day; it simply has been perfect.

Day 10

We wake at 7:30 but linger in the grassy meadow at Squaw Lake until noon, not wanting to leave. While at Squaw Lake, we have our first and only dispute on the JMT. I want to shampoo my hair, as I try to do every four days in the backcountry. My shampoo says "herbal" and "organic" but not "biodegradable." Jacobus says that is insufficient; if soap is not labeled "biodegradable" it will not decompose fast enough and may leach into streams, lakes, or groundwater. I promise to wash my hair in a pot more than 200 feet away from any water and argue that all soap is biodegradable, that my shampoo probably will degrade just as fast as the soaps that label themselves "biodegradable." Jacobus says I don't need to wash my hair after only four days. He touts the fact that he and the kids in his summer youth wilderness program didn't wash their hair for three weeks and were fine. I agree not to wash my hair today but reserve the right to wash it later if my head itches too much. I admire his dedication to protecting the wilderness in its natural state and hope my hair can last three more days.

The dispute resolved, at least for the time being, we start climbing to Silver Pass (10,900 feet), which our guidebook describes as having "breathtaking views." We hike swiftly, pass impressive Chief Lake, and reach the top of the pass in 50 minutes. The book's description is accurate and Jacobus is so motivated by the views that he takes eight photos in an attempt to capture the 360-degree panorama.

From the top of the pass it's all downhill, 3,200 feet in fact. Passing several alpine lakes, including Silver Pass Lake, we then ford Silver Pass Creek and stop for lunch. At lunch, I see the huge pack I met three days earlier coming down the trail, grab my camera, reintroduce myself and ask if I can photograph "the largest pack I've ever seen." I don't want anyone to think I am making this up. He asks, "Have you met the German guy who barely speaks English and who's trying to set a Guinness record?" "No," I reply. "Well, he's trying to hike the JMT both ways in 14 days. He's carrying no bear canister, no tent, no stove or pots, no utensils, and no sleeping bag. He says it takes too long to roll and unroll a bag and to get undressed to get into a bag, so he just sleeps with all his clothes on, wrapped in just a wool blanket," he adds. I ask when he and his two hiking buddies plan to finish the JMT, and they say September 27, a week before us. This surprises me, as we've been walking at about the same pace. They say they wish they had another week, like us, but have to get back to work and would get fired if they stayed away longer. Too bad for them. I wish them the best as they depart, but I have my doubts they will finish the JMT.

The descent continues, often very steeply, down the loose, rocky, west wall of the North Fork of Mono Creek canyon. The trail is spectacular, but the steep steps are tough on knees. My trekking poles earn their keep on this descent, as they cushion the downward steps on this very rockiest of trail sections. Several groves of aspens are passing sights; the smaller trees are just beginning to turn yellow but the large ones are completely green. We enter the Mono Creek drainage, cross the creek—easy in September, but possibly quite dangerous in early summer—then walk along the creek as it descends to the Main Fork and Quail Meadows, where Jacobus and I will camp. At 7,700 feet, this is one of the lowest spots on the JMT. We cross the Main Fork of Mono Creek on a steel footbridge and camp on the south side of the creek.

After a wash, it's time to watch the alpenglow on some large puffy clouds floating above us. Jacobus cooks Mountain House Chicken Stew for dinner, which we both rate a keeper. It's been a moderate day, but tomorrow will be the toughest yet—11+ miles and 4,000 feet of elevation gain. We both bed down early in hopes of getting a good night's sleep before our 7 a.m. alarm.

Day 11

I wake up at 3 a.m., can't get back to sleep, and lay in my sleeping bag until it begins to get light at 6:30. Jacobus wakes up a half-hour later and we hit the trail at 9:15 a.m., the earliest start yet. Jacobus says he would like to walk ahead this morning to see how he handles the initial 2,300-foot climb, so we agree to meet on the top of Bear Ridge at the first junction, at 1 p.m. He soon is out of sight, and I start up the switchbacks, which our guidebook describe as "never-ending." Counting the switchbacks, I lose count at 40; there must be well over 100 of them. Instead, I begin to concentrate on my Walkman, Marvin Gaye singing in my ears, encouraging me to dance up the trail, and the beautiful thick forest—cottonwoods, white fir, aspen, Jeffrey pine, red fir, silver pine, mountain hemlock, and, near the top, lodgepole pine. The aspens, in particular, are captivating, big-trunked and beginning to turn yellow and gold, with leaves trembling in the breeze.

I establish a hiking rhythm and plan to take a rest break when my altimeter shows I've climbed 500 feet, but I keep going. I pass 1,000 feet elevation gain and keep on until 1,800 feet, stopping then to have a Powerbar and look back toward Silver Pass. After 10 minutes or so, a young woman from New York City catches up with me and stops to talk. She has just finished hiking the 180-mile Tahoe to Yosemite trail and now is doing the JMT. She looks super-fit and strong and we talk about hiking and the World Trade Center tragedy. All in her family are safe and accounted for. Soon, her hiking companion, a young woman from Atlanta, catches up, and they resume climbing, while I consume a Barbara's crunchy granola bar. I take off 5 to 10 minutes after the women leave but catch them about 10 switchbacks later. I'm really feeling strong today and am flying up this mountain. Up ahead, Jacobus is taking a break waiting for me. I continue on ahead as Jacobus talks to the two women, arriving at the junction at the top of Bear Ridge not at 1 p.m., but at 11:55 a.m. It's my best hiking effort yet and merits Jacobus' comment, "You were quite impressive on that climb, Dad," when he reaches the top.

The two women join us for lunch at the top of Bear Ridge, but as soon as we're all seated on the ground and eating, Jacobus jumps about three feet in the air, grabs his crotch and yells, "A damn bee bit me on my right nut!" As he goes hopping down the trail, the women and I break into laughter at his pain and embarrassment. It seems the salami we have been eating for lunch attracts yellow-jackets, commonly known as "meat bees." After this, we try to keep the salami inside of a plastic bag as much as possible. Later in the day, his nut still in pain, Jacobus presents me with the prospect of surveying to find the stinger he thinks is lodged there. I politely decline, suggesting instead that he try Apis, a homeopathic remedy for bee stings. He takes my advice, and his symptoms quickly recede.

The trail descends 1,000 feet to Bear Creek, a delightful flow of water over exfoliating granite, with innumerable good swimming holes. We climb alongside Bear Creek for about three miles before undertaking a 1,200-foot climb to Rosemarie Meadows. A fine campsite with wood set up inside a fire pit just waiting for us to light a match has been left by a thoughtful backpacker. Jacobus and I build a wonderful but small "Indian fire," and keep warm on a cold night at high altitude. It has been the longest, hardest hiking day yet, but I feel like Mother Pollard, a famous civil rights activist, who once said after a day of marching in Alabama, "My feet are tired, but my soul is rested."

Day 12

Up at 7 a.m. on a cold morning, I mope around waiting for the sun to hit the campsite. Today's hike will be 11 miles, 1,500 feet of elevation gain and 3,500 feet of elevation loss to reach Muir Trail Ranch by 4:30 p.m. There Jeanine is expected to arrive by helicopter. I'm still tired from a poor night's sleep two days earlier and feel like taking a nap at breakfast. But, motivated to meet Jeanine on time, I push myself up the trail, past the islanded, beautiful Marie Lake and over Selden Pass (10,900 feet).

From Selden Pass, the trail descends past several lakes, including Sallie Keyes Lake, where Jacobus and I try to take naps. Bothered by some yellow-jackets, I'm unable to nap, so I hike ahead. A mile up the trail, I encounter about 10 horses grazing nearby. As I pass, one runs directly at me and chases me around several trees before giving up. I don't know if the horse is trying to be friendly or aggressive, but I'm not about to stand around to find out. My adventure over, it's on to Senger Creek, where Jacobus catches up. We break out lunch, sharing it with two cowboys and their horses. They have stopped to let the horses drink from the creek after a stiff climb from Muir Trail Ranch. One of the cowboys thinks that the horse that chased me probably was "just playing around."

From Senger Creek, it's a 3,500-foot descent on long switchbacks, mostly exposed to the sun, but with fine views of Blayney Meadows and the river valley, formed by the South Fork of the San Joaquin River. The valley walls are punctuated with colorful yellow aspens. The long descent is hard on my basketball-damaged knees, and near the end of it I'm almost crawling, but Jacobus and I make it to Muir Trail Ranch and walk another mile to Blayney Meadows, where the helicopter will land. After a 20-minute wait, we hear the sound of a copter coming up the canyon. It passes overhead and proceeds up the river and out-of-sight—do they know where to land?—but it soon returns and spots the meadow. Jeanine is the first to step out of the copter, and she runs to me, her face beaming, and gives me a big kiss and hug. It's great seeing her, well worth pushing myself to get here today, and I don't feel tired anymore. The pilot explains being nearly two hours late was the result of delays by the Federal Aviation

Administration in giving permission for flights following the World Trade Center incident.

Jeanine's friend Jennifer is with her, along with two very large suitcases, two large duffle bags, two backpacks and a refrigerator-container of fresh food—the sum of their gear and our resupplies. There is no way to lug this much stuff up the trail to camp a mile away, so we decide to camp near the meadows. A woman comes by, introduces herself as Linda Ross, a landowner in this area, says it is OK to camp here, and tells us, "The horses in the meadow shouldn't be a problem, but stay away from the black stallion with the white, diamond-shaped, spot on his nose. He can be a devil."

We set up camp and all cook dinner together, the first fresh food I've had on the trail. Then I read my journal of our first 11 days on the trail to Jeanine, Jennifer, and Jacobus. Tonight I will sleep with my wife.

Day 13

We all sleep in until 9. As soon as breakfast is completed, Jacobus and Jennifer hike to a hot springs a mile away across the South Fork of the San Joaquin River. As they leave, Jennifer says, "We'll leave you two lovebirds alone to mess around while we're gone." I rise to the occasion.

Jacobus and Jennifer return three hours later, we organize and pack our new supplies, eat lunch, then leave for the hot springs without a care in the world. We pass through Muir Trail Ranch on the way to the hot springs and stop to talk to the proprietors. Muir Trail Ranch, a group of wooden cabins, a dining room, and horse stables, has been in this location for over 100 years. Its right to continue operations was grandfathered into the 1964 Wilderness Act, as were the in-holdings of several medium-size ranches in the area. The ranch operates only in the summer as lodging for groups of up to 14 people, who can rent the whole ranch for a week at a time. It also provides services to backpackers, who, for a fee of $45, can mail supplies to the ranch.

From the ranch, we cross the river, find a hot springs in a lovely meadow near the river, and soak in the 102-degree water for an hour. Upon our return to camp, we see five horses, led by the black stallion, rummaging through our gear. Jacobus and I run at them, yelling and screaming and waving our towels, and they run away. The camp is a total mess and we survey the damage. Our four-pound Stephenson Warm-Lite tent has been trampled; the nylon is ripped and one of the two supporting tent poles is destroyed. We will have to carry the 7½-pound North Face tent that Jeanine and Jennifer brought for the rest of our hike. Our gear is spread out all over the campsite and all the gear is covered with dirt and yellow horse-slobber. Fortunately, our backpacking food had been sorted and put inside our bear canisters, and the horses were unable to break inside. They did, however, find my vitamins in a nylon bag, and while they did not break through the bag, they chewed it. My supply of vitamins has been reduced to powder, so for the next week I will be eating vitamin powder, not tablets. Our fresh food, left in a nylon refrigerator container which the horses succeeded in breaking open, had been eaten. I also had left my pack open and all my gear is out of the pack and on the ground. All my clothes are full of dirt and horse-slobber and small items such as lip screen, boot weather-proofing, shampoo and toothpaste are destroyed. Even my book has been chewed by a horse—I hope he was searching for knowledge.

We clean up, wash clothes, and hang them to dry overnight. Then we barricade the campsite with logs, cook two of our freeze-dried dinners, and go to bed. We are asleep for a couple of hours before we are awakened by the black stallion and a brown horse trying to break into our camp again. Jacobus and I spring out of our bags, find rocks nearby and throw them at the horses. They retreat, but an hour later are back, and we run at them, throwing rocks, before they run away. This time, Jacobus and I collect a pile of rocks and two heavy sticks in case they return again. And, return they do, three more times, before we are able to nail the black stallion with two well-placed rocks, one in the hindquarters and the other in the neck. Even then, the stallion lurks in the forest 100 feet away snarling at us and rising on its hind legs and kicking its front legs wildly in the air until Jacobus and I chase him deep into the forest yelling and throwing rocks. The landowner's description of the stallion as "a devil" has proven accurate.

We are prepared for bears but didn't expect to be attacked by horses!

Muir Trail Ranch to Grouse Meadows

Day 14

After a night with little sleep, Jacobus and I awake grog-
gy at 8, make breakfast, and carry Jeanine and Jennifer's
gear to Blayney Meadows for the 10:30 helicopter pick-
up. But the helicopter doesn't arrive until 12:30 p.m. The
pilot explains he was delayed by fog in the S.F. Bay Area.

We say goodbye, hike a mile to the Muir Trail Ranch,
thanking the owners for their permission to land the helicopter nearby, then take the short lateral trail to re-join
the JMT. We walk three miles along the South Fork of the
San Joaquin River before reaching the junction with the
Piute Trail and a bridge over Piute Creek. During our stop
for lunch on a smooth rock along the creek. Jacobus
wades in the creek, while I try to take a nap to catch up
from the missed sleep last night.

After lunch, we cross the bridge, leaving the John
Muir Wilderness and entering Kings Canyon National
Park. Our walk leads along the South Fork of the San
Joaquin River through a splendid canyon that's full of yel-

low and gold aspens both along the trail and up the sides of the canyon walls. The river is spectacular, a series of cascades over exfoliated granite into calm pools, interrupted by occasional waterfalls. It would be easy to spend a whole day swimming in these waters and sunning on the smooth rocks.

Next we cross the river on a steel bridge and then recross it a half-mile later on a log bridge. This is where the JMT turns east and the Goddard Canyon/Hell For Sure Pass Trail continues south along the river. The late start prevents us from reaching Evolution Meadow, the planned destination, so we find a pleasant campsite along the river near the log bridge. Jacobus and I will have to make up a little distance tomorrow. Our bags laid on the ground, we watch the stars shining brilliantly through the trees before quickly falling asleep.

Day 15

Today is the last day of summer, and the weather remains perfect. The day begins with a brisk 1,000-foot climb to Evolution Meadow, first up switchbacks amid yellow and gold aspens, then along Evolution Creek, which is even more spectacular than the South Fork of the San Joaquin River was yesterday. We pass a series of 10- to 30-foot waterfalls that drop into beautiful green pools of water, interspersed with long cascades over smooth granite. Too bad we're behind schedule and can't just jump in. We continue on toward Evolution Meadow.

When Jacobus and I reach the top of our climb, we encounter Ken and Eric, two of the 80-pound-pack guys we met several days ago. "Have you seen Everett?" they ask anxiously. Apparently, he became separated from Ken and Eric two days ago and are now backtracking to Muir Trail Ranch and Florence Lake looking for him. I comment, "I hate to think something bad might have happened to Everett, but on your way back, you should check the cascades and waterfalls in Evolution Creek. Everett liked to swim the creeks and it is possible he could have slipped and hurt himself in one of those cascades." If he had, he could be dead.

Twenty minutes later, we run into the Colby Meadow ranger, Dave Gordon, a tall, thin, fit man in his late 40s or early 50s, who is looking for Everett. He asks us what we know, including whether he was getting along with his hiking partners, and records everything we say in a journal. Dave has radioed ahead to rangers farther south on the JMT, telling them to be on the lookout, and we promise to have Everett contact a ranger if we find him. Dave has been the summer ranger in the Evolution Basin for about 15 years and knows everything about the area. He says that if we had been here a month ago, "you would have seen 50 to 60 people a day here. In September, it's just five to six a day." Actually, since September 11, it's been more like one a day, and once we pass Dave, we hike through all of Evolution Basin, one of the most popular and beautiful areas in the Sierras, and see no one.

After lunch alongside Evolution Meadow, one of the largest meadows in the Sierras, we walk to McClure Meadow, find some cascades and a pool in Evolution Creek, take off our boots and clothes, and jump in. The dip in the cool water is the perfect elixir to me, as I then climb 1,600 feet to our destination, Evolution Lake (10,850 feet), where once again we are all alone in a gigantic alpine lake basin. The best campsite in the area, on the tip

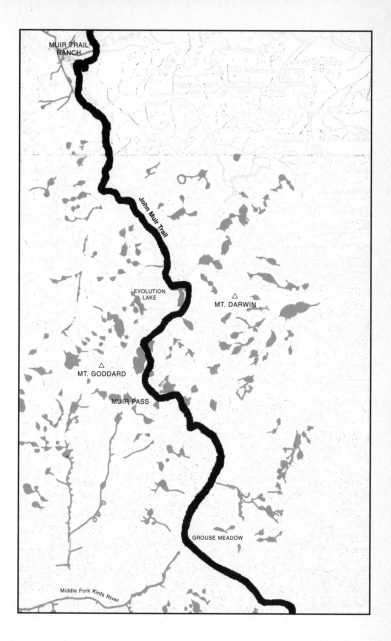

of a little peninsula extending out into the lake, is all ours. The campsite is beyond spectacular, and Jacobus says, "This is the best yet!" Then he jumps in the cold lake for a swim.

Another perfect day; another night of a million stars. Jacobus and I now have hiked more than half our distance and climbed approximately 27,000 feet of elevation gain—more than half the estimated 50,000 feet of elevation gain on the JMT. We are on schedule, my body is holding up fine, and I feel nothing can stop us except a resupply screw-up or some terrible weather, which doesn't seem likely. Nothing at all for us to worry about, we can just enjoy each day and its challenges.

Day 16

Today is the first day of fall, but the Indian summer continues.

After Jacobus takes another swim in Evolution Lake, we reluctantly leave our splendid campsite and hike toward Muir Pass (11,955 feet). At beautifully blue Sapphire Lake, we meet ranger Dave Gordon. He's talking to a backpacker by the name of Baja Verde (a.k.a. Richard Green). Dave informs us that Everett has been located. He's not behind his hiking partners but three days ahead, at Rae Lakes, where he tells the Rae Lakes ranger he will wait for his buddies "for a half-day," then hike on. Of course, this means that his buddies will never catch up with him, as they have backtracked a day and a half and are now five days behind him. And, since they backtracked looking for him, it is unlikely they will be able to finish the JMT. They have to be back to work on September 27 and will be unable to hike 115 miles in six days. Everett has been separated from his buddies for four days, yet has failed to check in with any of the four rangers stationed between Muir Trail Ranch and Rae Lakes, all of whom have radio phones. He has walked past messages left on the trail for him by four rangers. We're all glad to hear that he is alive and well, but Dave's characterization of him as a "doofus" seems apt.

As we walk, I notice Dave is reaching down and shoveling horseshit off the trail. I ask him about this. Dave says, "I hate seeing horseshit on the trails, so I try to remove as much of it as I can. The horse packers won't do it, so I do it." This is a noble enterprise that's going well beyond his job description, and Dave is the first person I've ever seen do it. So, when you hike the JMT section between Muir Trail Ranch and Muir Pass, expect a clean trail, at least as long as Dave Gordon continues to be the backcountry ranger for this area.

Hiking on toward Muir Pass, we have a conversation with Baja. He turns out to be quite an adventurer having traveled extensively throughout the world. Baja is 55 years old and appears to be in great shape at 6'1" and 170 pounds. A physical therapist from Mesa, Arizona, Baja aspires to live in Patagonia, provided he can persuade his girlfriend, who wants to live in southern France. Many years ago, the former Richard Green took a difficult bicycle trip in Baja California, which his friends advised him against and ended up with a broken collarbone. Since that trip, he's been Baja Verde, an inspiration to the hikers he leaves behind.

Baja is hiking the JMT in 13 days and carrying just a 35-pound pack, including his food. To save weight, he has brought a one-pound bivy sack instead of a tent, a lightweight 40-degree sleeping bag, a minimal amount of clothes, and no bear canister. He sleeps with his food, but to avoid bears never sleeps where he eats, on the theory that bears will most likely smell cooked food but not his uncooked food. After dinner, he hikes a mile or so and finds a site where no one has camped recently so there will be no food scents, and hangs his smelly socks nearby to emit non-food odors. So far, he has not been bothered by bears. If his socks smell anything like mine after a day of hiking, I can understand why. Of course, this system requires that he camp in less-desirable areas and sleep in a bivy sack more cramped than a coffin, but that's his system, and he's sticking to it.

On the way up Muir Pass, Baja asks my occupation. I was a civil rights lawyer for 25 years and, prompted by his many questions, tell a few litigation war stories, which he seems to enjoy. He asks, "What do you do now?" I reply, "Here I am," and he says, "Yes, here you are, reaffirming that you are alive." A pretty good way of stating it, I think. I ask, "Why are you here walking the JMT?"

"It's beautiful," he answers. "I've wanted to do it since I was 15 growing up in Long Beach, and I've never done a long hike. I wanted to hike the JMT to see the Sierras, but also to find out if I can hike 200-plus miles. It's kind of a mid-life crisis thing. It reaffirms I'm alive." At a pace of 18 miles a day, I'd say Baja is alive and passing the test.

At the top of Muir Pass, we spot Dave Gordon and Sandy, the Le Conte Canyon ranger, and all have a few laughs about the exploits and misadventures of Everett and his buddies. Jacobus and I check out Muir Hut, a block stone hut erected by the Sierra Club in 1930 in honor of John Muir and his contributions to saving wilderness, and take photos. Clouds begin to cover the sun, the wind starts to blow, and the temperature quickly drops 20 degrees. Mother Nature is saying, "Okay, you guys, the weather has been great, but I just want to remind you that this is the first day of fall and I'm in charge." We acknowledge her supremacy by putting on warm clothes and heading down the pass.

Jacobus has been blown away by the beauty of the hike past Sapphire and Wanda lakes and up and over Muir Pass. The hike down is just as rugged, rocky, austere and beautiful—but harder on my knees. We descend 1,500 feet, where we spot Baja waving to us and shouting, "Come and join us, we've got a nice campsite big enough for all of us." He's with Kevin, another hiker who joins us for dinner and an evening's conversation, all enhanced by a pipe with a little vegetable-matter in it. Kevin hiked the Pacific Crest Trail (2,600+ miles) in 1999 and now is re-hiking the portions he liked best. I ask him, "Of all the PCT, which part is your favorite." "This is it—the JMT," says Kevin, "and McClure Meadow"—which we had passed the day before—"is my favorite single place anywhere on the whole planet."

Kevin's knowledge of the PCT is of great interest to Jacobus, who hiked 250 miles of it in Washington three years ago, and it turns out they even know the same post-master in Stehekin, a small town in Washington along the PCT. Kevin will be leaving for two months of trekking in Nepal on October 14, and he asks about my experiences there four years ago. We stay up late talking.

It's nice being out here with a bunch of long-distance ("through") hikers. There is no sense of competition, just a common bond and understanding about why each of us has chosen to hike 200+ miles and/or spend a month or more in the wilderness. We all intuitively understand this and little need be said. Although we may speak with each other only for a few minutes, or sometimes share a campfire or a meal, we're all brothers and sisters in our love and passion for this magnificent stretch of wilderness. I feel a spirit here much larger than Jacobus and myself. It is the power of the mountains, lakes, streams and meadows, and also the collective spirit of the people sharing this hike during a glorious September. We are all blessed, and know it.

Day 17

Baja, camping just five feet away, is up at 6 a.m. and has his stove buzzing by 6:30. He does his best to be quiet, but it's hard to make a gas camp stove quiet. He leaves around 8. Kevin, who prides himself on his late starts and long hiking days, competes with us to see who will be last to leave camp. Jacobus and I win, leaving at 11:15. It's a relatively short day, mostly downhill, descending into the glacially carved Le Conte Canyon. The trail is partially blasted out of rock and parallels the Middle Fork of the Kings River and its dramatic and steep cascades. Expansive views of the canyon and Big and Little Pete meadows in the valley below, all accented by yellow, gold and red foliage, mostly aspen and red mountain heather are highlights.

Our hike continues past the Le Conte Canyon Ranger Station and crosses the Dusy Branch of the Kings River descending from Dusy Basin. Dusy Basin brings back memories of a 10-day hike I had taken many years ago in October with my friend Bill. He had to leave and return to work after seven days, while I went on for three days by myself, exiting the Sierras via Bishop Pass and camping at Dusy Basin in preparation for our hike over Bishop Pass the next morning. Bill had taken our tent, and when it snowed in Dusy Basin, I was huddling inside my warm bag next to a little rock wind-break. Two other back-packers nearby were camping in a large three-person tent. They were a honeymooning couple from Los Angeles, and I didn't think sharing their shelter would be exactly what they had in mind. I just got deeper into my bag and avoid-ed the snowfall. At daylight I rose, ate a quick dry break-fast, packed up and, as the weather deteriorated, began to hike out toward Bishop Pass.

I passed by the couple's tent to say goodbye, and the woman was beginning to ask herself why they had chosen a Mammoth Mountain condo. "I'm very worried about getting over the pass today. Would you lead us out?" I replied, "I'm worried, too. You two at least came over that pass getting here, but I've never been over Bishop Pass and I'm very concerned about the storm. Visibility already is poor and the weather is getting worse. If the weather dete-riorates any more, we could have trouble finding the trail over the pass. But getting over the pass should be easier for you because you've done it before." "Well, I know we did it once, but I have no confidence that my husband can find his way back in these conditions, so please wait for us," the woman replied. I thought, "This is their honey-moon, and already she's lost confidence in this guy." Against my better instincts, I agreed to help them. It took an hour to get them packed up.

The weather continued to deteriorate, and I had to walk at their slow pace up the pass—a hike made neither faster nor more pleasant by her oft-repeated complaints about her husband's "idiotic plan to go backpacking on our honeymoon." The episode was beginning to sound like an installment of the famed *Ladies Home Journal* series "Can This Marriage Be Saved." By the time we reached the top of Bishop Pass (12,000 feet), we were in near whiteout conditions, with heavy snow and strong winds. In such weather, passes can be quite dangerous, as it is possible to get started down the wrong direction, then reach (or fall over) a precipice. I told them to sit in one spot and not move, while I looked for the correct route down. After 20 minutes I found the trail down the other side, and it was a safe descent. I've often wondered how long that marriage lasted. My guess is about two months.

The weather today is fabulous; no snow, just all sun and blue sky, a good day for going over Bishop Pass, to be sure, but so much better to be continuing south on the JMT.

Jacobus and I pass a drift fence above Grouse Meadows that our horse-packer, Greg Allen, had described to me a month ago. [A "drift fence" keeps stock from drifting too far during their grazing.] We set up camp along the river at a large horse camp and wait for Greg, owner of Rainbow Pack Station, to arrive with resupplies. Expecting him to arrive at 4, Jacobus and I are there at 3 and eat lunch. By 5:30 p.m., we're beginning to get nervous. Contingency plans are made to hike out over Bishop Pass tomorrow if our supplies do not arrive. The "attack of the horses" back at Muir Trail Ranch has left us no spare food. The prospect of hiking an additional 26 miles and twice crossing a 12,000-foot pass doesn't exactly thrill us, but at 7:15, just as dusk is setting in, I hear horses and someone calling, "Mr. Saperstein?"

Greg arrives with his brother-in-law, John, and three

pack horses and introduces himself. Greg and John quickly and efficiently unpack the horses, set up camp, build a fire, and begin cooking a classic cowboy dinner—two steaks that look like they weigh about two pounds each, baked potatoes and baked corn. Greg offers us some of everything, but we stick to our Mountain House freeze-dried lasagna and one of two ginger bread cakes Grandma Faye has sent in our resupplies. Greg's offer of two Miller Lites is gladly accepted though. I didn't think Miller Lite could taste this good.

After dinner Greg and John and Jacobus and I all chat around a nice small campfire until 10:30. Greg is an interesting fellow, not a cowboy by heritage, but a city-dweller from Southern California, who decided with his wife, Ruby, two years earlier, to break out of the city by doing something radically new and different. With no background with horses, let alone the horse-packing business, they bought the run-down Rainbow Pack Station at South Lake, outside of Bishop. Greg spent most of his first year cleaning out 10 tons of horse manure, which had been left in environmentally damaging areas, and repairing the pack station buildings and equipment. I ask John what the family thought when Greg and Ruby did this, and John says, "We all thought they were nuts."

"How could a city-dweller learn to horse-pack and run a pack station," I ask, and he says, "I learned by doing. Mostly, it's just common sense." He also explains his non-violent approach to managing his animals, a change from the prior ownership of the pack station, and how much smarter, sure-footed, and playful his mules are compared to the horses. When questioned about the practices of some of his fellow horse-packers, he admits some of the old practices had been insensitive to the environment, but that most horse-packers were trying to do a better job now.

Greg supports the Sierra Club and packed for many Sierra Club Hi-Light trips this year, but complains about two local environmental groups who oppose all horse-packing. He also complains about some Forest Service "overregulation" but admits that, although the Forest Service was tough on him at first due to the poor reputation of the prior owners, they recognize that he is trying to clean up past abuses and do a good job. I ask John, "What does the family think of Greg and Ruby's decision now?" and John says, "We think they're going to make it."

I ask Greg what time they plan to get out tomorrow morning and he says, "8 or 9." I say, "Please don't leave before Jacobus and I shave, so you can pack out the shaving gear. We only get to shave once a week." Then it's good-night and to sleep with the soft light of the campfire illuminating the surrounding trees.

Grouse Meadows to Rae Lakes

Day 18

Greg and John are up at 7:15, and so are we. Jacobus and I finish packing our outgoing box, trying to lighten the load as much as possible for the remaining 90 miles, which promise to be the hardest and highest. I dump my Therm-A-rest chair, thus saving 11 ounces, and Jacobus dumps his ground tarp, which weighs 10 ounces. But, since we've added some warm clothes, zero degree sleeping bags, and a 7½-pound tent, the packs actually are heavier than at the start of the trip.

For breakfast it's the standard oatmeal breakfast, while Greg and John build an open fire and cook biscuits, pork sausages and oatmeal for themselves with genuine "cowboy coffee"—coffee grounds boiling on the bottom of the pot. The percolator is for wimps and city-folks! I sample half a cup of coffee, which tastes good if a bit chewy. Greg offers us each a couple of pork sausages flavored with maple syrup. It's the kind of food I normally never would consider eating, as the sausages contain a lot of fat and sugar, but out here they sure taste good. The sausages just drip with some much-needed fat. Maybe I

GETAWAY GUIDE TO THE JOHN MUIR TRAIL

won't be a single-digit body fat person by the end of this trip after all.

Jacobus and I talk with Greg and John around the campfire nearly the whole morning. Some of Greg's politics may not match mine (he's home-schooling his kids in part because he thinks UNESCO has taken over the American educational system), but he and John are fine men. Greg is working hard to run a clean and environmentally responsible pack station and is trying to make his trips accessible to paraplegics. Greg tells us several stories about taking paraplegics into the wilderness on horses and how excited he became when they saw places they never thought they could get to. He vows to do more for the disabled, even fighting with the Forest Service for the right of disabled people to bring motorized wheelchairs into the backcountry. "The Americans with Disabilities Act was passed to open up opportunities for disabled people, and I'm not going to let the Forest Service screw it up," he says. Maybe Greg's real calling is not as a horse-packer, but as a civil rights attorney for the disabled!

The conversation lasts until 11:30 a.m., and they don't get out of camp until 12:15, well past their 8 to 9 departure plan. They have enjoyed talking with us as much as we have enjoyed talking with them.

Today is a planned layover, but we decide to make up the time lost when we spent a day at Mammoth Lakes watching TV coverage of the World Trade Center. Keeping the original schedule, we'll be out of the mountains by October 4. Our plan is to reach Truckee that night, Jacobus and I will be able to play in a golf tournament there the following day. Besides, we don't need a rest day.

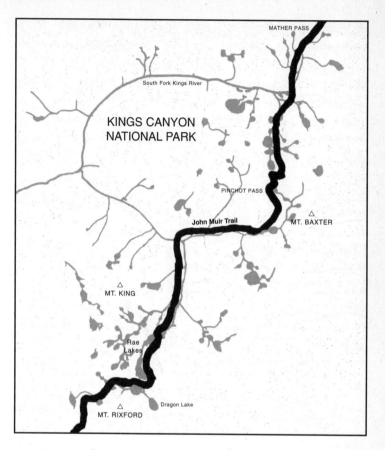

Hitting the trail with the heaviest packs yet carried, Jacobus and I soon are climbing alongside Deer Creek toward the day's destination, Deer Meadows. The trail is completely unpopulated (except for one middle-aged woman we meet who is hiking the California portion of the Pacific Crest Trail by herself with a horse). After walking for a couple of hours, I round a bend and encounter a little meadow with the most delicate, soft color palette. I see a carpet of lush, ungrazed brown-green grasses, brown

141

bushes with fading red leaves, green pine trees with fallen brown pine cones at their feet, gray-green sage bushes, white bark on the aspens and brilliant yellows and golds on the quaking aspen leaves—all bathed in bright sunshine. The scene is like a great impressionist painting, and I wish Guy Rose or Joseph Raphael, or another of the great California impressionist painters, were here to capture it, allowing me to take it home and remember it forever.

After finding a nice campsite next to the creek and setting up camp, Jacobus and I go for a swim. Jacobus remains by the creek soaking up rays in the warm sun and I catch up on my journal before Jacobus says, "Want to learn some rock games?" Never one to pass up such opportunities, I join him at the creek. There, we throw stones at various objects floating in the water until the sun is about to set and we have to cook dinner. This is like being a kid again. How wonderful it is to have the time and leisure to throw stones in a stream—and to have a fine companion to do it with!

Day 19

The sun hits our tent at 8 a.m. and I get up to wash my face in the creek. I sit quietly, watching the water careen off rocks, creating infinite variations of shapes and forms, and the sun reflected in thousands of facets of the water. Loren Eisley once wrote, "If there is magic in the world, it is in water." He must have watched a stream like this. John Muir called it "champagne water," an apt description. Yes, it will be nice to wake up in the morning and take a hot shower at home, but that experience will lack the magic of splashing my face in a mountain stream.

Jacobus gets up, and I tell him how much I've been enjoying the streams, creeks, rivers, and lakes on this trip. He says, "I know what you mean. That's why the first thing I do each day is to go to the stream or lake to pump water. It's just a great way to start the day."

The bulging packs are still heavy and full of food as we head off toward Upper Palisade Lake (10,880 feet) via the Golden Staircase. The Golden Staircase was the last portion of the JMT to be completed, much of it blasted out of rock. Kevin warned us it was the steepest section in all the PCT, and it's true. The Staircase is filled with thousands of large blocks of granite that Jacobus and I must step up and over and is the steepest hiking we've yet encountered on the JMT. Jacobus calls the steps "brutal" and the full sun and sparse shade don't make it easier, but we keep trucking at a good pace. Near the top, around a bend and over a rise, the view is a high point of our Sierra journey. Looming ahead is a vertical rockwall formed by the Palisade Crest, a number of 14,000-foot and near-14,000-foot peaks (North Palisade, Middle Palisade, Disappointment Peak, Mt. Bolton Brown and Mt. Prater).

The cliff walls of the white and gray granite canyon we're hiking in, with the huge rock-wall looming high above, is the most awesome sight we've seen on the JMT. No one who sees this could ever question why the Sierras are called the High Sierras. Walter A. Starr, Jr., author of the *Starr's Guide,* wrote in 1934, "For me, the grandest view in all the Sierra" is from one of these peaks, the North Palisade. This is the heart of the High Sierras; California has 15 of these majestic 14,000-foot peaks, and we've entered the region that has 14 of them (the 15th is Mount Shasta, 200 miles to the north, which is a volcano and a part of the Cascade Range, not the Sierras). There are more peaks to come and Jacobus and I look forward to seeing them all.

At the top of the Staircase are the Palisade Lakes, Lower and Upper, and the goal is to reach Upper Palisade Lake tonight, so I keep hiking, listening to Clifford Brown on my Sony Walkman Memory Stick. Brown plays his composition "Parisian Thoroughfare" and I think of Leon and how much he would enjoy this hike. But, he did the right thing staying in Paris and pursuing his career. We'll all do another long hike together along the PCT some day.

On a granite bench 250 feet above Upper Palisade Lake, Jacobus and I set up camp near an alpine stream with a beautiful 10-foot waterfall, where I pump some filtered water for the night. After dining, we turn in early planning an early start. Tomorrow we climb Mather Pass (12,100 feet). As Jacobus turns off his light for the night, he says, "I'm really stoked about climbing Mather tomorrow."

Day 20

The Sapersteins' string of 19 straight days of perfect weather comes to an end. During the night, it rains, hails, and even snows a little, and the wind gusts to 40–50 mph. The tent is wedged between rocks and whitebark pine and handles the weather, but I don't sleep well.

The morning breaks windy, but dry, with clouds crashing off the walls of the 12,000- to 14,000-foot rock faces around us. We are climbing Mather Pass today a bit concerned about a storm and possible lightning over the pass. But my barometer has dropped only a tenth of an inch, from 20.30 to 20.20, so I predict, "This looks

Top: Vidette Meadow with Forester Pass in distance (page 154)
Bottom: Trail up Forester Pass (page 159)

*Top:Trail carved out of rock on north side of Forester Pass
(page 159)
Bottom: Approach to western side of Mount Whitney (page 160)*

Top: Ascending last 1000 feet of Mount Whitney (page 163)
Bottom: Mission accomplished! Top of Mount Whitney (page 163)

Whitney Portal: End of the trail!

more like a rogue squall than a major storm." On that note, we put on our rain gear and head up. The wind continues to blow strongly, often catching my pack and throwing me sideways. This is very unpleasant, as the trail is narrow with some exposure. As the day progresses, the clouds dissipate and sunshine prevails. By the time we hit the top of Mather Pass (named for Stephen Mather, the first Superintendent of the National Park Service), it remains windy, but the clouds have nearly disappeared.

A sheltered cove at the top of the pass is a good place to stop for a snack. The views up here are superb—north to the Palisade Crest and south to the upper basin of the South Fork of the Kings River, Split Mountain (14,058 feet) and Pinchot Pass (12,130 feet), tomorrow's climb. Karen, a 28-year old woman from Florida who is hiking the JMT by herself, soon joins us. She hiked the complete Appalachian Trail (2,160 miles) last year in 7½ months. An environmental educator and youth leader, her resumé closely parallels Jacobus's. She enjoys hiking alone but finds the nights can be spooky. I ask what her next hiking adventure will be, and she says, "I'd like to hike the whole PCT, but it would be nice to first find the right man to do it with." She leaves the top first, but we catch up with her over lunch at the bottom of the pass and talk more before she takes off down the trail trying to make her 13-miles-a-day goal.

Jacobus and I continue down the trail to a pleasant campsite on the South Fork of the Kings River, take a soapless bath in the river, watch a fine sunset, and contemplate climbing another 12,000-foot pass tomorrow.

Day 21

I sleep 10 hours, but wake up with a very sore right ankle and a moderately sore left ankle. I must have turned them yesterday, but I have no idea when or how. In any case, I can't push off the ankles very well and am moving slowly, taking small steps on the steep uphill to Lake Marjory, a beautiful alpine lake at 11,132 feet, where I find Jacobus enjoying a swim. He hiked there in an hour and 10 minutes; I took two hours. We take a short Powerbar break and both watch the sun glistening on the lake—it is like watching 10,000 Christmas lights—then I head up toward Pinchot Pass (12,130 feet), named for Gifford Pinchot, the first director of the Forest Service, and John Muir's arch-nemisis on many issues, including Hetch Hetchy Dam. The dam flooded a beautiful glacial valley in Yosemite—Muir's most painful conservation loss. Approaching the top of the pass, I'm walking even slower, stepping over the rocky terrain, as my ankles are getting worse. I make it to the top of the pass in 3½ hours; Jacobus takes two hours.

After lunch at the top, taking in the inspiring views to the north and south, it's time to head down. After descending 500 feet on switchbacks, we enter an alpine zone of small streams and lakes set in a carpet of gold grass and shrubs. I continue to move slowly, and our arrival in camp along Woods Creek is at 6:15. We have been hiking since 10 a.m. and have covered only eight miles. After bedding down, I take Arnica internally and rub Traumel on my ankles, two homeopathic remedies for sprains and strains, and hope for a miracle.

Day 22

My homeopathic prayers are answered! I awake after 10 hours of good sleep with no pain in my ankles. I can take normal steps without wincing; I feel reborn.

We descend 2,000 feet along Woods Creek enjoying its waterfalls and cascades flowing down smooth white and gray granite shaded by yellow aspen groves. Some of the swimming holes are spectacular, but we have to keep moving to make our 10+ miles to Rae Lakes, and, hopefully, meet the horse-packer for resupplies. We have seen only four hikers in five days, but crossing Woods Creek on a bouncy, swinging suspension bridge (8,550'), the "Golden Gate of the Sierras," Jacobus calls it, a group of high school kids from Happy Valley School in Ojai, California, greets us. They are led by their very lovely Scottish leader, Annette Bering, in beautiful, long, reddish-blond braids. Annette asks me a thousand questions about our JMT hike and salutes us for doing it as father-son. We also talk about taking inner-city teen-agers into the backcountry. Her multi-racial high school kids had no prior experience with backpacking or wilderness and they struggled and complained at the beginning of their week-long, 45-mile, Rae Lakes loop hike, but now, on the fourth day, are doing great. They decide to make camp at the bridge and I tell them of some great swimming holes a half mile or so up Woods Creek.

From Woods Creek, the climb is moderate up the lightly forested canyon of the South Fork of Woods Creek, through stands of aspens, to a nice lunch spot. We chat for an hour and a half about Wilderness Volunteer Corps, the organization he works for in Seattle. WVC takes inner-city high school kids into the wilderness for three weeks at a time each summer to backpack and also spend a week working with the National Park Service or Forest Service building and repairing trails. It's hard work for anyone, but certainly for kids not used to physical labor in the backcountry. WVC also works with these kids throughout the year, providing help with their schoolwork and guidance as they pass through the difficult teen years. Jacobus tells how different kids react to the experience, ways he has handled different personalities and situations, and why the kids grow and mature through the challenges the backcountry experience presents. It is inspiring to listen to him and learn how Jacobus handles these kids and how they have benefited from the program. Jacobus always enjoyed a magical relationship with other children. He was almost a Pied Piper with kids, as they would instinctively gravitate toward him, following him and his activities wherever they led, even when he was only a few years older than they. Now, as an adult, he has not lost his charisma or leadership with kids. His leadership skills have grown and flourished. I am proud to be his father and am inspired by the positive impact he will have on children in the future.

We are enjoying sitting and talking, but Jacobus and I still have most of 2,000 feet to climb to get to Rae Lakes and must resume our ascent. After hoisting our packs, we move back onto the trail and keep talking for the next two hours while climbing steadily. The talk helps to take my mind off the elevation gain. Approaching Dollar Lake (10,200 feet), I faintly hear a cowbell and wonder, "Could this be our horse-packer?" We walk to the edge of a cliff overlooking the South Fork of Woods Creek to see where the noise is coming from. Down below, on the other side of the creek, is a cowboy, with horse and mule. I yell out, "Brian?" He yells back, "Guy?" Our horse-packer has arrived. Through shouts back and forth over the sound of the fast-moving cascades of the creek, we determine that our supplies have been left in one of the bear boxes at Rae Lakes and that Brian will be by at 8 tomorrow morning to pick up the stuff we are discarding.

Hastening on, we find our stuff in a bear box located at the most beautiful campsite in the Rae Lakes—an area often described as the most beautiful lake basin in the Sierras. We open our cardboard boxes and begin sorting out the new supplies. Everything is here—new batteries, toilet paper, Grandma Faye's pinwheel cookies, some clean clothes and our food for the rest of the trip—but after everything is laid out, Jacobus notices there are seven breakfasts and seven lunches but only two dinners. We are going to have to shift some of our dining plans.

So we will forego our planned layover day at gorgeous Rae Lakes and continue the hike to Mt. Whitney, thus saving one's days worth of food. This means hiking 15 days without a break, but we both hiked strongly today and can go on. With two dinners left over from the last section, we will use our extra oatmeal and granola for the remaining dinners. Not an ideal menu, but with the abandoned layover day this will be enough food to complete the JMT.

We stay up late organizing supplies, then to bed with a five-day old Sunday New York Times and San Francisco Chronicle that Jeanine has sent in the supply boxes and stay up until midnight reading. The sports news is great— Oakland A's clinch wild-card slot in the American League playoffs, Barry Bonds hits home runs 65 and 66—but the world news is worse than dismal. World Trade Center disaster, possibly 5,000 people dead, plans for war against Afghanistan, stock market down 15 percent, economy tanking and so on.

Rae Lakes to Mt. Whitney
and Whitney Portal

Day 23

Up early to meet Brian Berner, who arrives promptly at 8 a.m. to pick up our stuff. It's a short conversation as he has a long day ahead and needs to get going. As he is packing up his mule, I ask him how long he's been packing. "This is my 29th season." Jacobus asks, "How have things changed in that time?" "It's gotten a lot worse," Brian replies. I ask, "How?" "Over-regulation by the government. This area used to be completely open to grazing stock, and we were allowed to bring in groups of 500 people with 500 stock. Now, groups are limited to 18 people and we can't graze animals in places like Rae Lakes." Looking at this exquisitely beautiful and fragile lake and meadow environment, I try to imagine what it would be like with 500 people and 500 animals, while hoping that Brian gets his horse and mule packed up before they defecate in our kitchen, where they are standing. Mercifully, the horse, mule and Brian leave before any of them crap in our camp.

Today's hike is past the three Rae Lakes, each more

beautiful than the last, with Fin Dome looming above, and then up Glen Pass. The packs are heavy with a full load of food, and we move slowly as I try to keep up with Jacobus. The trail on the bottom half of the climb is steep and loose, but the switchbacks on the top half are better, and, aided by the driving blues of Jimmy Thackery playing in my ears, I finally make it to the top (11,973 feet). Jacobus says Glen Pass was the hardest yet due to the weight of his pack.

A descent of 1,600 feet along austere granite walls and then past Charlotte Lake, where our family once took a memorable horse-packing trip. Jacobus was about 4 and Leon 7. Jeanine and I didn't think we could get them deep into the backcountry by ourselves. We had the horse-packer at Onion Valley take us the 12 miles into Charlotte Lake. He left us there for a week, then returned with horses to pick us up, called in the packing business a "spot trip." Jacobus was too young and inexperienced with horses to have his own, and the packer put him on the back of mine. Since my horse had to carry two people, they gave me the biggest horse with the widest back. Not a good idea, as I am not too flexible (my yoga instructor used to call me "Mr. Stiff"). Spreading my legs to accommodate such a wide-back horse caused me great pain and distress—so much so, that when we stopped for lunch, I refused to get off the horse, saying, "If I get off, I'm never getting back on." In any case, we had a little adventure when the horse got away from me in a meadow approaching Charlotte Lake and galloped to the lake, with Jacobus screaming and bouncing on the back. There, the cowboy had to lift me off the horse, as I was physically unable to move my legs, which had become stiff boards extending

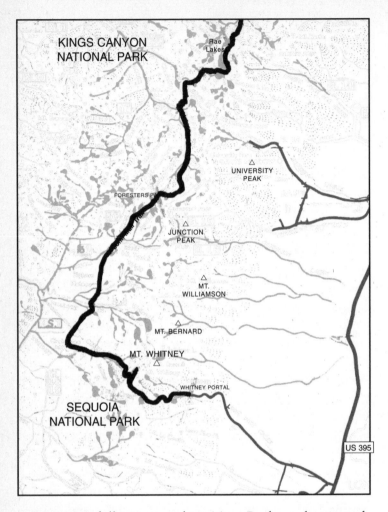

out in a painfully unnatural position. Back on the ground, I staggered around in a hilarious Groucho Marx crouch-walk for an hour before attempting to sit down. The cowboy stayed overnight with us before getting ready to return the next morning, and, as he was packing up his horse, I went over and said very quietly, "You know you are supposed to return seven days from now to pick us up. Well, I don't want you to return, we'll just walk out." "But it's too late to get your money back," the cowboy protested. I explained further, "I didn't ask for my money back. All I ask is that I never see those horses again!" I didn't share this new information with my family until two days before we were scheduled to be picked up by the horses. Then, I said, "We've had a change of plans. We're going to hike out." There were no objections, which would have been futile at that point anyway, and we hiked out in two days. You could say horses and I are not compatible.

After descending from Glen Pass, the trail side-hills around Mt. Rixford, passes through Bullfrog Meadow, then enters the Bubbs Creek drainage and Vidette Meadow. The hike down to Vidette Meadow offers a huge panoramic, post-card view of Center Peak, Center Basin and the formidable Forester Pass (13,200 feet) in the distance, framed on the east by Kearsarge Pinnacles and on the west by dramatic East Vidette peak. Down to Lower Vidette Meadow (9,650 feet), where we camp alongside Bubbs Creek and greet Karen, the woman from Florida we met a few days earlier on Mather Pass. Karen tells us of her plan to climb Whitney at night, stay to watch the sunrise and fly a kite she has been carrying for 200 miles, an unusual way to end the JMT hike. I salute her for her romanticism and imagination.

Day 24

We invite Karen to take a side hike with us today to Center Basin, but she is intent on getting over Forester Pass. We wish her well. Jacobus helps me wash my hair with a pot this morning, the first shampoo in seven days. Then we leave for a three-mile hike to the junction with the Center Basin Trail and a side hike to Center Basin in the afternoon.

Jacobus and I climb for about an hour and a half and reach an unmarked trail going east. As we stand there reviewing our map and pondering whether this is the trail to Center Basin, Erika Jostad, the Crabtree Meadow Ranger, comes by with her husband. They are hiking out to Cedar Grove to attend an Emergency Medical Training refresher course. Erika confirms that this is the trail to Center Basin and encourages us to take it. "Center Basin is wonderful," she says. Erika says she has been a back-country ranger for nine years and will be spending the winter at Mt. Rainier as a seasonal ranger. Her jobs all are seasonal, so she is constantly applying for NPS jobs and moving around among national parks. Her husband tries to stay close to her by working on trail crews.

Our talk continues for 45 minutes about a variety of topics. She tells us the giardia danger has been "heavily oversold." "I've been drinking water from the streams with my Sierra cup for years without a problem." Her husband adds, "I've been working out here repairing trails with a crew of 40 men. We've all been drinking right out of the streams, without filtering water, and none of us has had any intestinal problems." I sure would like to believe the water is safe to enjoy the sensual pleasure of dipping my cup into a flowing stream and taking a big drink of fresh water. Sucking filtered water through a plastic tube just isn't the same.

I tell Erika we are headed to Whitney and ask if there are any bear boxes beyond Crabtree Ranger Station, and, if not, whether it is safe to camp above Crabtree without bear canisters. Our bear canisters were taken out by our horse-packer at Rae Lakes. Erika says, "This time of year, the bears are at lower elevations, so your food should be safe from bears, but watch the marmots at Guitar Lake and at Trail Crest, where you will leave your packs while you climb Whitney. The marmots love salt and have been chewing pack shoulder straps. Turn your packs over and cover them with something." This is new information for me and I thank her for the warning. I'd hate to lose my shoulder straps and have to carry my pack like a suitcase!

Does Erika know much about the origins of the JMT and why there are "original," "traditional" and "current" versions of the trail? Erika says she believes a private citizen initiated the idea of a trail from Yosemite to Mt. Whitney that would follow the Sierra crest and commemorate John Muir. The original JMT just patched together existing trails and did not always follow the crest. As time went on, new trail has been built to honor the original concept of following the Sierra crest, and older portions of the JMT were abandoned. Her husband tells about some of the construction, saying, "You won't believe the trail on the south side of Forester Pass; it was drilled and blasted right out of rock. If you look at the south side from below, you wouldn't even believe a trail could go up that rock wall, but it does. Men were hanging in harnesses on that wall to build the trail."

After saying goodbye to Erika and her husband, Jacobus and I eat lunch, set up camp near the Center Basin Trail, and take off for an afternoon hike to Center Basin. Next a climb up a rough, steep trail for 1½ miles, talking non-stop, and we arrive at a large alpine basin, full of small lakes, surrounded by 12,000- and 13,000-foot-plus peaks. We pick a lake, find a granite perch next to the water, and sun-bathe and swim in the lake. The scene is enchanting—blue alpine lake, with meadow and fall foliage on the banks, surrounded by jagged peaks. This spot is exactly the place where Richard Kauffman took the cover photograph for *Gentle Wilderness,* the large-format Sierra Club book about the Sierra Nevada, with text by John Muir. It is one of my favorite books and I've long wanted to see this landmark.

Jacobus mentions that the beauty of the Sierras reminds him of the desert. I had not really thought of the southern Sierras as a desert environment. But the dryness of the climate, the starkness and austerity of the jagged mountains and some of the colors of the meadow grasses and alpine plants are desert-like. I say, "I think you are right. We're very far south, Death Valley is directly to the east, and we're in the rain shadow of the Great Western Divide, a big ridge of 13,000-foot Sierra peaks to the west. It does seem like a quasi-desert, but if it is a desert, it is a desert paradise because of all the lakes and streams created by winter snowfall."

As sunset approaches, we walk back to our camp. Once there, Jacobus says, "Dad, the hike to Center Basin is the highlight of our trip for me." We bed down early, hoping to get an early start tomorrow. The formidable Forester Pass (13,200 feet) lies just ahead.

Day 25

Arising at 7 and out of camp by 9:15, early for us. As Jacobus sprints ahead, I begin to settle into my hiking rhythm. Ten minutes out of camp, I hear a "hello" from my right and turn to see a tall man in an NPS ranger uniform calling to me. "Are you the JMT hiker who wants to know whose idea the JMT originally was?" he asks. I say, "Yes, that's me." "Erika Jostad called me on my radio phone yesterday, said she was unable to answer some of your questions and asked if I could answer them. Well, the man who originally proposed the JMT was Theodore Solomons." The Charlotte Lake Ranger is George Durkee, whose name I immediately recognize as the one on all the "No Fires Above 10,000 Feet" signs.

George says he has been a backcountry ranger for 32 years and knows quite a bit about the history of the Sierra Nevada and the biology of the area. He recommends reading Francis Farquhar's book, *The History of the Sierra Nevada,* and the book *Pathways to the Sky,* as well as his articles on the Yosemite Association website, www.yosemite.org. He also says Dawson's Books, in North Hollywood (where I grew up) has a great collection of books on "Californiana," including the Sierras.

We talk about horse-packers and some of their attitudes. I tell him about my conversation with Brian Berner, and George says, "We have a few good packers, but the old guard packers like Brian Berner think they own the national parks and should be able to do anything they want. In fact, for a mere $50 a year, they get to run trips and let their stock eat thousands of dollars worth of grass. They're here to make money, not to protect the land. They should realize that conserving the land protects their own businesses, as it keeps these areas desirable for their clients. One packer recently complained to me about closing down a meadow where the grass had been eaten down to half an inch from the ground. He said, 'But George, that last half inch of grass is the best part for the horses!' His idea of a meadow must be dirt."

After chatting with George for more than half an hour,

it's time to start up Forester. I excuse myself to try to catch up with Jacobus, who now is far ahead. At a brisk pace, Frank Sinatra singing in my ears, I move up the mountain as it transitions from whitebark pines to alpine meadows and lakes, and then into a vast alpine bowl with vertical rock faces on 13,000-foot-plus peaks to the east, west and south. Many people had told me how tough Forester Pass is—nobody had mentioned its beauty. The views are big and dramatic. I want to take photos at nearly every bend of the trail, but with only one roll of film to last to the end of the JMT, I conserve.

Forester Pass is not nearly as difficult as advertised. True, it is 1,000' higher than any pass we've yet climbed, but the trail is well-contoured and well-maintained. And the beauty of the scenery pushes thoughts of the elevation gain out of my consciousness. I'm enjoying every minute of the climb, thinking, "This is the most beautiful pass on the JMT." Jacobus waits for me to enjoy a Powerbar break where the trail travels along a thin ridge at 12,000 feet with great views in all directions, then takes off for the top, making it 15 minutes before me. At the top, I ask, "What do you think of Forester Pass now?" He says, "It's the most beautiful pass we've done!"

After a lunch at the top (13,200 feet), we leave Kings Canyon National Park. Sequoia National Park is next as we begin to descend the steep south side of the trail, the section blasted out of rock. It's a wonder that anyone was able to build a trail on this sheer rock face. We drop about 600' on switchbacks, then walk slightly downhill for four miles along the west bank of Tyndall Creek through a gigantic alpine basin, catching our first glimpse of Mt. Whitney to the east. The end of the JMT is in sight in the distance! Also in the distance are four animals moving toward a ridge; through binoculars they appear to be big horn sheep.

Shortly after passing the side trail to Lake South America, we locate a campsite with a bear box and set up camp alongside Tyndall Creek cascading beautifully over exfoliated slabs of granite. It has been a long and exhilarating day of hiking and another day seeing only one other person.

Day 26

Today is a transition day between Forester Pass and Mt. Whitney. To get in position to climb Whitney, we need to hike at least 10 miles today, to Crabtree Ranger Station. If still strong at the end of the day, and there's time, we have the option of continuing on to Guitar Lake, 2.9 miles past Crabtree and 1,000' higher on the route up Whitney. But Guitar Lake will be colder, windier and populated with those notorious pack-strap-eating marmots.

We ford Tyndall Creek and begin a climb before the trail takes an up-and-down traverse of the east side of Kern Canyon to Bighorn Plateau. Bighorn Plateau is a stark, arid, wide-open plateau at 11,000 feet with giant 270-degree panoramic views of the Kern Trench, Great Western Divide, and Kaweah Peaks Ridge, a view that equals any we've seen on the JMT. So there's a photo and snack stop before descending for an hour and a half to Wallace Creek, for lunch and naps on a grassy bench alongside the creek. At Wallace Creek is a junction with the High Sierra Trail, which I've considered hiking. Seventy-two miles long, it goes west to east from Giant Forest, along the Kern River and eastward to the summit of Whitney—a hike for another trip.

It's been threatening rain all day. Though walking in

sunshine, we see rain showers to the south, west and east. Crossing Wallace Creek, and switchbacking up the hill heading south, the trail seems to be leading right into rain. Jacobus is far ahead, so I stop for a Powerbar break at Sandy Meadow. Rain sprinkles the meadow, still bathed in sunlight. I watch for a while, then head east on the trail, with light rain following 10 feet behind. We have been blessed with phenomenally great weather for nearly four weeks, but this is almost surreal!

Crossing Whitney Creek and turning north toward Crabtree Ranger Station, walking away from the rain, it soon is no threat. At the trail junction to Guitar Lake and Crabtree RS, and, assuming Jacobus has hiked toward Guitar Lake, I head in that direction, but after a half mile realize I'm not seeing his footprints in the dirt and head back. There he is, wading in Whitney Creek. A wash up in the creek, into our warm clothes, and we cook dinner, resolving to get up by 7:30 and on the trail by 9:30 for our big day tomorrow—the conclusion of the JMT. We'll have to hike 13 miles, climb approximately 4,500 feet to the top of Mt. Whitney (14,494 feet) and over Trail Crest (13,700 feet), then descend 1,700 feet to Trail Camp, our longest, hardest day. But the packs will have only three days of food, and that will make the day easier.

Day 27

Up on schedule, we leave camp at 9:15. The sky is deep blue, but hiking east toward Mt. Whitney and above tree-line, the wind picks up, clouds cover the sun, and the temperature drops 20 degrees. On with a long-sleeve shirt— one of only a few times I've had to wear a shirt while hiking. Beautiful Timberline Lake (11,100 feet), with fall colors around the edge of the lake and Mt. Whitney reflected in the water, is a fine sight.

Jacobus is ahead of me, but waits at Guitar Lake (11,400 feet), which sits amid rock falls in an alpine meadow. A quick shared snack, then we begin the real climb among talus slopes switchbacking up the west side of Whitney, looming high above. A long, intimidating climb, but I catch a second wind, get into a good rhythm, and make it to the junction (13,480 feet) of the trail to the top of Mt. Whitney with only one short rest stop. Jacobus is waiting at the junction and we have lunch there, looking back at the trail just climbed and the outstanding panorama to the west. We talk with a young couple who have just climbed Whitney and are heading west to Crabtree, then put on some extra clothes, batten down the hatches on our packs so the marmots won't eat any pack straps or break inside for food. Then we begin climbing toward the summit and the conclusion of the JMT.

I climbed this trail 29 years earlier with Jeanine and Leon, when Leon was just five months old. I don't remember the summit climb being particularly difficult, but today the hike is hard. Even without my backpack, I'm tired and moving slowly through the starkly beautiful, rugged landscape of huge blocks of granite, often piled on top of one another in dramatic towers and shapes. It takes me nearly 1½ hours to hike the 2.2 miles and climb 1,200 feet to the top. Near the summit, clouds cover the sun, the temperature drops to about 35 degrees, and the wind picks up. But the sight of the Smithsonian summit building and Jacobus standing at the top causes a wave of jubilation, completion and success to drown out my tiredness. I walk the final 200 yards, hug Jacobus and exclaim,

"We've done it! No matter what happens on the way down, no matter what happens tomorrow or the rest of our lives, we'll always be able to say, 'We hiked the John Muir Trail!'" Jacobus says, "Dad, I want you to learn a new word. It's a word I've been saving for this moment. It is an Inuit word, 'nuanaarpuq,' and it means, 'To take extravagant pleasure in being alive.' Can you say it with me?" And we both say "nuanaarpuq" many times. It is the most perfect word for how we feel at this moment.

On the summit by ourselves! There is no one even to take photos of us. We perch our camera on a large rock, set the timer and take photos of ourselves and the phenomenal views in all directions. At 14,494 feet, we are higher than anyplace in the continental United States. To the north, is the serrated ridge of the Sierra Crest, with Mt. Russell (14,085 feet), Mt. Carillon (13,552 feet), Tunnabora Peak (13,565 feet), Mt. Barnard (13,990 feet), and Trojan Peak (13,960 feet); to the east, the Owens Valley, nearly 10,000 feet below, often called "The Deepest Valley," as it is surrounded on two sides by 14,000-foot mountain ranges, the town of Lone Pine and our route past Trail Camp, Mirror Lake and Lone Pine Lake to the trailhead at Whitney Portal, more than 6,000 feet below; to the south, Mt. Muir (14,015 feet), Mt. McAdie (13,799 feet), Mt. Mallory (13,850 feet), and Mt. LeConte (13,960 feet); and to the west, Mt. Hitchcock (13,184 feet), the Hitchcock Lakes and the route we've taken to get here past Whitney Creek, Crabtree Meadow, Guitar, Arctic and Timberline lakes, the Great Western Divide in the distance, and the beginnings of a spectacular sunset.

We'd stay longer, but it's getting even colder, particularly on my bare legs, so we sign the summit register (I sign my name and add the comment, "I almost bonked today, but I completed the hike up Mt. Whitney and the JMT!"), and head down at 5:30. The sun is dodging in and out of the clouds as it sinks lower on the horizon. By the time we reach our packs at 6:30, a great mountain sunset sits on the ridge of western mountains, extending at least 100 miles north and south.

When the sun sets, it gets very cold very fast, so we scramble to put on warm clothes and our headlamps for the hike down to Trail Camp at 12,000 feet. The bottoms of my toes feel like sandpaper, but, in my haste to head down, I try to ignore them. This proves to be a mistake. I have hiked for 27 days with NO blisters—how could I possibly get blisters now, after completing the JMT?

Next we climb 150 feet to the top of Trail Crest (13,700 feet), which marks the line between the east and west sides of the Sierra Crest, and then head down in darkness along a sometimes narrow trail, with a 1,500-foot fall-off on one side. There is a full moon tonight, but heavy clouds conspire to cover it just when it's needed, forcing me to rely on the headlamp and batteries now used for 15 days. Jacobus breezes ahead, undaunted by the poor light and 1,500 feet of exposure, but I descend slowly, hobbled by developing blisters on seven toes and slowed by the thought of stepping off into oblivion at any moment. Jacobus, sensing my concern, waits for me and offers his much brighter headlamp, then stays close as we inch our way down the pass. It takes me two hours to descend the 2.2 miles to Trail Camp (12,000 feet) and each step is painful. By the time we reach Trail Camp at 9 p.m. and I'm hobbling around, taking 6- to 12-inch steps.

At Trail Camp, the place is full of tents. Everyone is in bed so they can arise early to climb Whitney. The clouds have disappeared and the rocky landscape of Trail Camp, with Mt. Muir and Mt. Whitney looming almost directly overhead, is bathed in moonlight. After camping by ourselves for most of a month, here tents are lined up among the rocks like a backpacking condominium complex. We find a slot and set up camp. Both too tired to cook dinner, I eat the remaining supply of turkey jerky in my sleeping bag hoping that the hikers we're surrounded with don't get up too early, or are at least quiet. For the blisters, I sterilize a needle with a match, prick my seven toe blisters, hoping they will drain overnight, before conking out for the night.

Day 28

As expected, people arise early. At 4 a.m., rising to pee, I hear the four backpackers camped next to us getting started on their day. They are extremely quiet making breakfast and packing up, whispering softly, so I soon get back to sleep.

Not so quiet, however, is a group of three women across the trail from us, who wake me at 5:30 banging pots and talking loudly. I listen for a while, reluctant to get up in the cold, but when they start telling stories about how they each get constipated for the first few days of every backpacking trip, I lean out of my tent and yell, "I don't think anyone in camp is really interested in your constipation problems. I know I'm not. Do you think you could talk more quietly?" They quiet down for a while, then re-commence talking loudly, banging equipment, and laughing, I finally get up at 7:30.

I put on my jacket, grab my journal and pencil and

walk over to the women. "Excuse me, ladies. Do you think you could give me your names?" "Sure, but why?" one responds. I explain, "My son and I just finished hiking the John Muir Trail, and I've been keeping a journal, which I hope to publish as a book. I've been recording not only the hike, but also people we meet along the trail. I'd like to include the three of you." At this, they all brighten and smile and one of them says, "Really? You'd put us in your book? What would you say about us?" "I would say that in 31 days on the JMT, the three of you are the most rude and inconsiderate people we've met. I asked you politely at 5:30 to please talk more quietly, but that didn't seem to have much effect on you." "Well, we didn't know you were talking to *us*," one of the women responds. "Sure," I say, "there were a lot of people nearby talking about their constipation issues at 5:30 this morning!"

The three of them don't make a sound until they leave camp at 9:15.

There's another problem this morning. I'm out of toilet paper, and the modern, solar-powered bathroom at Trail Camp, which I've heard about and was counting on, has been closed due to backpackers dumping their garbage and non-biodegradable items. Jacobus encourages me to try his system using rocks and sticks to wipe, but a chapter from Carlos Castaneda's *Journey to Ixtlan* is a worthy alternative.

Jacobus has another idea this morning that I receive more favorably. To help the blisters, Jacobus suggests keeping my socks off and exposing the toes to the sun as much as possible. "The air and sun will dry out and harden the blisters and you'll be able to walk on them," he advises. Good advice. At camp until 12:30, I expose my toes to the air and sun. Then I tape them up with two thin layers, put on my boots, throw on the pack and hope not to hobble down the trail like yesterday, as we have 3,700 feet to descend to Whitney Portal.

The 6.2-mile hike to Whitney Portal turns out to be surprisingly beautiful, and my blisters are no impediment to the descent.

We leave Trail Camp and immediately begin descending over a wide and rocky trail following Lone Pine Creek and its many cascades and waterfalls. The views are to the east, where we see the V-shaped canyon framing the town of Lone Pine, Owens Valley and the Alabama Hills. Many Hollywood cowboy films were made in the 1930s to 1960s in the Alabama Hills, with simulated gunfights among the large rocks. Leon, Jacobus and I once spent a week exploring the Owens Valley when they were young, a trip that included a day of running around the Alabama Hills with toy squirt guns pretending to shoot at each other hiding in the rocks. Not PC maybe, but a lot of fun.

Our hike goes past Consultation Lake (11,680 feet). Water from the outlet of the lake plunges down a steep canyon southeast of the trail. The trail switchbacks steeply down to Mirror Lake (10,650 feet), with Thor Peak (12,300 feet) rising dramatically from the lake. Soon after Mirror Lake, the trail fords Lone Pine Creek and levels out as it passes through the meadow at Outpost Camp and its many campsites. As we descend, there are more backpackers climbing to Trail Camp for the overnight on their way to climb Whitney, hikers out for just a day hike to one of the lakes and even a hiker who started at 3 a.m. and climbed Whitney in a day—21.4 miles and more than 6,000 feet of elevation gain and loss. Many ask where we are coming from and when we tell them we just hiked the JMT, virtually all of them say, "I want to hike the JMT someday, too." I hope many of them will.

It's a brief climb after leaving Outpost Camp, then a descent to the junction with the trail to Lone Pine Lake and a stop for lunch, with Lone Pine Lake visible from the junction. We eat lightly, anticipating a cheeseburger and fries at the café at Whitney Portal, just a few miles distant. Beyond this junction, the trail becomes a series of long switchbacks as it descends moderately through a pine and chaparral forest to the trailhead at Whitney Portal (8,361 feet), where I sprint across the finish line. We've made it!

Looking back wistfully at the trail, I am reminded of the words of John Muir:

> Here ends my forever memorable first High Sierra excursion. I have crossed the Range of Light, surely the brightest and best of all the Lord has built; and rejoicing in its glory, I gladly, gratefully, hopefully pray I may see it again.

We walk over to the nearby café, order our cheeseburgers and fries, then phone a shuttle service to pick us up for Lone Pine, where we will spend the night before flying to Truckee—and Jeanine. The shuttle service can't pick us up for an hour, so we finish our burgers on the café patio, then hitch a ride into town. We get picked up by a Swedish hiker who has just hiked to Whitney and back in one very long day. After talking with him about hiking the JMT, he drops us off at the Best Western motel in Lone Pine, where we rejoin what passes as "civilization." We take a swim in the motel pool, call home, walk a mile into Lone Pine for a beer and dinner at a Mexican restaurant followed by a stop at the local saloon, which has a table shuffleboard game. Jacobus and I used to be accomplished at this game, once even getting to the finals of a tournament at the Triple Rock Saloon in Berkeley. Tonight, he whips my butt and I demand a rematch, but fare no better. Then we stroll the mile back to our Best Western. Tomorrow, by plane in an hour and a quarter we will re-trace the trail that took a month to walk. It's a month no plane ride will ever match!

Postscript

Including a few short side-hikes and the hike from the top of Mt. Whitney to the trailhead at Whitney Portal, we each have taken approximately 750,000 steps, hiked 236 miles and climbed more than 50,000 feet of elevation—twice the elevation gain of climbing Mt. Everest from Lukla, the traditional starting point—while walking through some of the most beautiful mountains in the world. I've lost 10 pounds and the two of us have had a wonderful time together, not just as father-son, but as friends. I have learned a lot about Jacobus, how he has matured since he last lived with us full-time, how competent and relaxed he is in the wilderness, and how much depth he has as a person. The trip has been successful by any measure.

The hardest part of the trip for me turns out to be returning to civilization. While it was exciting to have completed the JMT, I didn't really want to leave this paradise. The trauma of the World Trade Center tragedy, and the changes and complications to our lives that event would cause, certainly had something to do with my feelings. But it was much more than that. It was losing the purity and order of life on the trail. Everything we needed on the trail was contained in two backpacks. The simplicity of our daily routine—a leisurely breakfast, breaking camp and packing up, getting on the trail and walking, the joy of feeling muscles working, propelling me up the trail. The daily excitement of seeing and doing things along the trail I didn't expect—a beautiful cascade and an unplanned swim, an inviting meadow not shown on the topographical map, an approachable deer, a soaring hawk, a shallow lake in subtle shades of greens and blues, the sun reflected in water like thousands of twinkling Christmas lights, the alpenglow of sunset lighting high peaks and floating clouds, a quiet campsite in an alpine basin with views of a 13,000' granite rock wall reflected in a lake. It was losing the quiet of the wilderness, a quiet framed by the rustling of wind in the trees, the sound of a stream rushing over rocks, a quiet that allows you to absorb and appreciate every moment of the day. And it was losing the sensuality of the wilderness, the feeling that I was a part of everything around me, that I walked the trail, my hands and body brushed the trees, felt the cool freshness of the water, rolled in the softness of meadow grasses and reached out and touched the high peaks and granite faces. Telling this to my friends Bill and Jose, they both say exactly the same thing, "You touched the Tao." Sitting at my desk opening mail and rummaging through emails is a poor substitute for these experiences.

One of the most rewarding endeavors is getting ahold of pieces of nature in my mind—learning nature's smells and moods, sharing a view, thinking about how many steps the next pass or hill will take, wondering where a trail leads or a creek winds, or which topographical contour lines on a map will be the most interesting to visit. Knowing nature like this is the best kind of ownership, the most indelible, the most permanent. It feels good to say, "Now, I know the John Muir Trail," or "Now, I know the Sierras." But, of course, I don't. What I know better is myself, and the JMT and the Sierras have helped. In 1877, John Muir wrote, "In every walk with nature, one receives far more than he seeks . . . These beautiful days must enrich all my life. They do not exist as mere pictures . . . but they saturate themselves into every part of the body and live always."

Even the events of September 11 reinforced the power of nature. The destruction of the World Trade Center showed the impermanence of man's constructions. The Sierra wilderness has been around for 25 million years, but the constructions of man were destroyed in an instant. Challenged by the tragedy of September 11, nature showed me the healing power of wild places; walking in wilderness was simply the healthiest thing I could have been doing in that next month. The American public understands the connection of wildlands and the need to de-stress; in the two months following September 11, visits to our national parks increased 30 percent over prior years. More than a hundred years ago, John Muir wrote,

> Climb the mountains and get their good tidings. Nature's peace will flow into you as sunshine flows into trees. The winds will blow their own freshness into you, and the storms their energy, while cares will drop off like autumn leaves.

Muir's advice perhaps is even more relevant now than it was then.

The healing power of wilderness is not just spiritual.

Scientific research has shown that the air in the high country and around waterfalls is heavy with negative ions (oxygen atoms that have gained an extra electron) and that these negative ions have a positive effect on people's moods by increasing serotonin levels, leaving people feeling more alert, refreshed and uplifted. In fact, negative ion levels in mountain environments and near waterfalls can be 1,000 times greater than the atmosphere in inner cities. No wonder I felt so blissed-out after a month in wilderness!

The trip changed me and the way I look at my life. It has unmoored me from my routines, transformed the way I look at choices and encouraged me to accept challenges with greater confidence. A year ago, Jeanine, Jacobus, and I had been invited by some close friends to kayak the Grand Canyon on their private permit (which had taken them 12 years on the National Park Service waiting list to obtain). It is a once-in-a-lifetime invitation, but I do not have the kayaking skills to run such a big-volume river and became apprehensive about the trip the moment I said yes. Returning from the JMT, I abandoned that anxiety and ran the river the following summer. I realize that opportunities to do things like hike the JMT or kayak the Grand Canyon are experiences that cannot be missed, that there is no purpose in worrying about not succeeding, that the only productive thing to do is to practice, prepare and be ready to do the best I can. Furthermore, there is a whole range of trips I might not ever have considered but which now seem eminently doable. Already, I am planning to hike the Tahoe to Yosemite trail next September with Jeanine and my niece, Unmi, compete in the Tahoe to Truckee cross-country ski race, and am looking into a walk across England, hiking the Haute Route in the

French and Swiss Alps, climbing Mt. Aconcagua (23,000 feet) in Argentina, hiking parts of the Appalachian Trail and doing extended cycling trips in Utah, Montana, California, Italy and France. The youthful vitality, or the healthy knees, of 20-year olds are gone, but so what? There is enough fuel in the tank to do a lot of great things, and I'm not going to miss those opportunities.

Pieces of nature are indelibly in my mind now and I will never be the same.

Index

About the Author

Guy T. Saperstein is a 1960 graduate of the University of California and a 1966 graduate of the University of California Law School. The firm he co-founded became the most successful private civil rights law firm in America, litigating the largest sex, race and age discrimination class actions in history. Saperstein has been on the Board of The Sierra Club Foundation for eight years and is currently president of the foundation. He lives in Piedmont, California with his wife, Jeanine. His oldest son, Leon, is a fashion photographer in Paris, and his youngest son, Jacobus, is an environmental educator and outdoor trip leader in Seattle. Saperstein has been hiking in the Sierras since he was 11 years old.

GETAWAY GUIDES

Each of these guides is an ideal planner for short or long trips. Written by experts who visit every one of the places they recommend, the Getaway Guides can be used for long weekends, week-long trips or three-week grand tours. With recommendations for every budget, each Getaway Guide is years in the making to insure that your trip is a winner from start to finish. Selective and sophisticated, each book reveals the secrets travel writers usually reserve for their closest friends.

The Getaway Guide to Agatha Christie's England
by JUDITH HURDLE • TRADE PAPERBACK • 192 PAGES
ISBN 1-57143-071-7 • $16.95 ($21.95 Can)

The Getaway Guide to California
by ROGER RAPOPORT • TRADE PAPERBACK • 256 PAGES
ISBN 1-57143-068-7 • $17.95 ($21.95 Can)

The Getaway Guide to the American Southwest
by RICHARD HARRIS • TRADE PAPERBACK • 270 PAGES
ISBN 1-57143-073-3 • $17.95 ($21.95 Can)

The Getaway Guide to Colorado
by RICHARD HARRIS • TRADE PAPERBACK • 227 PAGES
ISBN 1-57143-072-5 • $17.95 ($23.95 Can)

The Getaway Guide to Washington
& Southern British Columbia
by RICHARD HARRIS • TRADE PAPERBACK • 240 PAGES
ISBN 1-57143-079-2 • $17.95 ($23.95 Can) • COMING JUNE 2005

Available at your local bookstore, or contact:
RDR Books • 2415 Woolsey, Berkeley CA 94705 • phone 510-595-0595
fax 510-228-0300 • www.rdrbooks.com • e-mail roger@rdrbooks.com